Ṭáhirih: A Portrait in Poetry
Selected Poems of Qurratu'l-'Ayn

The Martyrdom of Táhirih
by Tooraj Djahangirloo (1989)

STUDIES IN BÁBÍ AND BAHÁ'Í HISTORY
VOLUME SEVENTEEN

Táhirih:
A Portrait in Poetry

Selected Poems of Qurratu'l-'Ayn

Edited and translated
by Amin Banani

with Jascha Kessler and Anthony A. Lee

Kalimát Press
Los Angeles

Copyright © 2005 by Kalimát Press
All Rights Reserved

Manufactured in the United States of America

Library of Congress Cataloging-in-Publication Data

Táhirih : a portrait in poetry : selected poems of Qurratu'l-'Ayn /
edited and translated by Amin Banani
with Jascha Kessler and Anthony A. Lee;
p. cm.
Includes bibliographical references.
ISBN 1-890688-36-3 (hard cover)
1. Qurrat'al-'Ayn, 1817 or 1814-1852--Translations into English.
I. Qurrat'al-'Ayn, 1817 or 1814-1852. II. Banani, Amin, 1926-
III. Kessler, Jascha Frederick, 1929- IV. Lee, Anthony A., 1947-
PK6528.U77A23 2004
891'.5512--dc22   2004010445

Kalimát Press
1600 Sawtelle Boulevard, Suite 310
Los Angeles, California 90025

www.kalimat.com

kalimatp@aol.com
To order: orders@kalimat.com

CONTENTS

A Woman for Our Time
by Amin Banani
1

On Translating a Persian Mystical Poet
by Jascha Kessler
31

Editor's Note
39

The Poems

Look Up!
47

Just Let the Wind . . .
49

He Has Come!
51

Proclamation
53

The King Walked In
55

Start Shouting!
58

Morning Breezes
61

Point by Point
64

Your Brilliant Face
67

A Beauty Mark
69
In Pursuit
71
My Head in the Dust
73
Sleeper!
75
His Drunken Eyes
77
Lovers!
79
The King of Love
81
Listen!
84
Running After You
87
Friends Are Knocking at the Door
89
I Am Lost
92
This Heart
95
No One Else
97
From Those Locks
102

Notes to the Poems
by Amin Banani
109

A Woman for Our Time

by Amin Banani

ONE HUNDRED AND FIFTY YEARS AGO, in an obscure corner of Persia, a woman removed the veil from her face in a public gathering of men. This courageous act, which ultimately led to her execution, had an unprecedented impact on some outstanding men and women in Europe, on the Indian sub-continent, and in America. But in her own nation, most of what has been said and written about her since was intended to cover her over again with many layers of veils.

The reasons for all the obfuscation are easy to detect. Initially, the guardians of the order against which she rebelled did their utmost to deny her existence by use of slander, vilification, and accusations of heresy against Islam. Subsequent generations of Iranians, who may have been free of religious dogmatism and fanaticism, have tried to make a fairer judgment. They have, however, often been ignorant of the historical facts and have neglected the underlying values and the prevailing culture of their own society. They have forced alien and ill-fitting

Amin Banani

ideological preconceptions upon her life and times. The results are invariably incomplete and inaccurate. This volume allows her own voice—through her poems—to speak for herself, her time, and her motivations.

The Woman

THE WOMAN WHO WAS BORN in Qazvin in 1817 (some sources suggest 1814), has come to be known by many names. She was given the name Fátimih Zarrín-Táj at birth. But she is remembered best by the beautiful appellation Qurratu'l-'Ayn (Solace of the Eyes) used by Sayyid Kázim Rashtí, the leader of the Shaykhí School, and by the title Táhirih (Pure) given to her by Mírzá Husayn-'Alí Núrí, Bahá'u'lláh, a leader of the Bábí community and the subsequent founder of the Bahá'í Faith.[1] She died a martyr for her cause in 1852, strangled to death at night in a garden in Tehran by a drunken soldier carrying out his orders, her body thrown into a dry well and covered over with stones.

---

1. There is some uncertainty concerning when and by whom she was first addressed as Táhirih. An undated letter from the Báb calling her Táhirih is ascribed by some researchers as possibly dating from 1847. What is certain is that the appellation was used by Bahá'u'lláh at the Conference of Badasht in 1848, and thereafter it became her prevailing and preferred identity. She herself used it in some of her poems as a traditional pen name *(takhallus)*. Two further strong pieces of circumstantial evidence must be taken into consideration in support of Bahá'u'lláh's initiative in the use of the title: 1) it was at Badasht where Bahá'u'lláh also gave new titles to a number of other Bábís present and took the appellation "Bahá" for himself, and 2) in subsequent years, the Bábís and Azalís, both of whom opposed the Bahá'ís, but who naturally hold her in high esteem, overwhelmingly refer to her as Qurratu'l-'Ayn and refrain from using the name Táhirih.

A Woman for Our Time

She lived an eventful, rebellious, tumultuous, and heroic life and was killed at the age of thirty-six for her deeds and words. What has survived of her writings is a number of theological discourses, doctrinal disputations, and polemical tracts in affirmation of her new faith written mostly in Arabic prose—and a very small number of poems, mostly in Persian. This volume focuses exclusively on the latter. A clear distinction is implied, then, between her words and her voice.

Táhirih was—insofar as her family, her education, her social networks, and her social position defined her—a scholar of religion. A full account of her philosophical, doctrinal, and intellectual positions must include a painstaking and judicious examination and analysis of all her prose writings. But, it is her poet's voice that provides us with a portrait of her person and her passion. Of her extant works, the prose writings in Arabic and Persian are works of nineteenth-century religious scholarship that are too arcane and abstruse for the general public. A handful of poems, however, reveal her tempestuous temperament and make her accessible to all people at all times. That is not to say that she was deliberately autobiographical in her poems, or that she adopted any narrative scheme in her verse. This volume is, however, an attempt to present a portrait of Táhirih through her poems.

She was, first and foremost, a woman of action. Her words alone, were they not limned against the dramatic deeds of her short and stormy life, would give ample evidence of her revolutionary and pioneering character. But it is the resonance of her deeds and her words that brings into focus the heroic figure of Táhirih.

Her historical identity and the events of her life are well documented and have been recorded by friend and

Amin Banani

foe. And there is the rub. The foes have reviled and slandered her, and the friends have defended and beatified her. Except for a few recent treatments,[2] all the writing about her is either hagiographic or vituperative. She is depicted either as a saintly martyr, a cunning vixen, or a fiery feminist. The pious treatments—true enough so far as they go—underplay elements of her social and personal power struggles, while they gloss over profoundly meaningful, private choices in her life. The vituperative attacks are nothing more than the fanatical ranting of a patriarchal religious hierarchy startled and enraged by her encroachment on their monopoly of learning and her unveiled threat to their power. The strictly feminist revolutionary accounts, while bringing out an essential dimension of her historical impact, do so at the cost of compartmentalizing her personality, ignoring the context of her struggle, and distorting her motives. None of these is satisfactory. Only with the help of her poems can we hope to see through the layers of her profoundly complex and remarkably single-minded motivations.

The Poems

THE TOTAL BODY OF EXISTING POEMS attributed to Táhirih is not large. It consists of fewer than sixty short and medium length poems. Both the words "existing" and "attributed to" need further clarification here. Her short and tumultuous life, the beleaguered circumstances of

---

2. See, Abbas Amanat, *Resurrection and Renewal: The Making of the Babi Movement in Iran, 1844-1850* (Ithaca: Cornell University Press, 1989) pp. 295-331 and Farzaneh Milani, *Veils and Words: The Emerging Voices of Iranian Women Writers* (Syracuse University Press, 1992) pp. 77-99.

A Woman for Our Time

the Bábí community, the clandestine handling of Bábí manuscripts, the scattering of her possessions, and the hostility of her immediate family members, who may have destroyed or suppressed her papers—all these mitigate against any sense of assurance that we now have access to all the poems that she wrote. As late as the 1990s, a scholar in Baku, Azerbaijan,[3] made claims to have found some poems of Táhirih in Turkish: And neither the likelihood of validity of that claim (for Qazvin was, and still is, a bilingual region—speaking both Persian and Turkish) nor the lateness of the discovery are surprising. That we had not known of these poems or were not aware that she wrote in Turkish (as well as Persian and Arabic) is not in itself important. But we are forced to recognize, as a result, that we are nowhere near possessing, or even attempting, a critical, authenticated, and complete edition of her poems. The possibility of more poems turning up in such places as the attics of her family, or the basements of some lapsed descendants of early Bábís and/or Azalís, or even in the diplomatic archives of St. Petersburg cannot be ruled out.

The Classical Tradition

THE STUDY OF TÁHIRIH'S POEMS has been bedeviled by recurring controversies over attribution and authenticity. Here there are a number of cultural, historical, and socio-psychological forces at play. Insensitivity to these issues can lead to hasty, inappropriate, and incorrect conclusions. The questions of literary tradition and poetic originality

---

3. Aziza 'Cafarzada, *Zarr'intac Tah'ira* (Baku: Göytürk, 1996).

Amin Banani

cannot be discussed outside of the poetic legacy that Táhirih inherited and to which she made significant contributions. To arrive at a full appreciation of her poems, therefore, an overview of the long and rich history of Persian poetry is necessary.

The formal aspects of Persian poetry changed very little through a thousand years of Persian history. Before Táhirih ever put pen to paper, a rich, many-layered, and voluminous stream of Persian poetry had included such giant poetic figures as Attar, Saʿdi, Hafez, and Rumi. Poets expressed themselves within forms of poetry that were regarded as classical and traditional. Occasionally, the great poets might introduce innovations of language or theme or rhyme. Such changes gradually became accepted into the canons of poetic form and today have become familiar to Persian audiences. Although scholars of Persian literature might appreciate their uniqueness, the distinctive character of many poems that were once fresh and innovative in their own time is now largely lost. Almost all classical Persian poems were written within a strict tradition that insisted on conformity to certain forms, rhyme schemes, subjects, poetic vocabulary, and other rhetorical devices and principles.

In scope and impact, this Persian tradition was not confined to Persia proper. It was, indisputably, the preferred medium of poetic expression from Central Asia to Asia Minor in the west, and to the Indian subcontinent in the south. Even long after Turkish-speaking migrants settled and dominated the outer reaches of the Iranian world, Persian poetry remained as the acclaimed and accepted mode of literary creativity and expression.

The classical tools of *esteqbál* and *tazmin* are time-honored traditions of Persian poetry—much like the tools of theme and variation found in music. The first device, *esteqbál*, is the practice of writing a new poem patterned on the form and structure of a more famous earlier poem written by someone else. Here the poet deliberately imitates the formal aspects of the earlier poem in such a way that it should become immediately obvious to the knowledgeable reader which classic work she is making reference to. The second poetic device is *tazmin*: here the poet borrows a line from an earlier poem and incorporates it into a new poem. The borrowed line is usually found at the beginning of the new work, and it is used as a springboard for the poet's theme.

These are both common aspects of Persian poetry through which a poet may pay homage to earlier classical writers. At the same time, either of the devices may become the poet's own conceit, by which she calls upon a familiar line or image, using it to serve a new purpose which is entirely her own. The borrowed line, then, both pays tribute to the classical history of Persian verse and simultaneously announces the new poet's confidence in her own ability to match (or better) the work of the great Persian masters.

Our contemporary, romantic notions of uniqueness—by which artists claim to have given birth to a new and original work from no other source than personal inspiration—were utterly foreign to the Persian cultural tradition of Tahirih's time. Such ideas of uninfluenced originality were, in fact, unknown in Western art tradition until relatively recently. The great European artists before the eighteenth century—like the great Iranian artists—conceived of themselves as working within a tradition, copying the works of antiquity, daring to improve on the works of old masters. For example, Michelangelo himself,

Amin Banani

the greatest master of Renaissance sculpture, consciously sought to recreate the classical works of ancient Greek sculpture; and he conceived of his work as a part of that ancient tradition. He copied and openly borrowed from Greek masterpieces while enriching the tradition with his own style.

So, in classical Persian poetry it is commonplace to use a line from, or imitate the style or meter of, the poems of an earlier poet. Naturally, this approach can result in mere imitation, and many poems written in this manner are mediocre, uninspired, or even worthless. But, both *esteqbál* and *tazmin* can be used to good effect by great poets. The familiar lines may be used to surprise (even astonish!) the reader with the poet's new purpose and intent—so that the poem becomes both old and new, conventional and revolutionary.

The Survival of the Poems

TÁHIRIH'S POETRY HAD BECOME IMPORTANT in her lifetime. That some of her poems had currency among early Bábís is well attested. Nabíl-i 'Azam, the Bahá'í historian, records that in 1848, on the march from Badasht to Mazandaran, she composed some verses with a refrain. These she chanted from her howdah[4] while she rode on one side and Quddus on the other, as she taught the Bábís accompanying her on foot to chant out the refrain in unison—a veritable traveling cantata on two and four feet.[5] 'Abdu'l-Bahá recalls in *Memorials of the Faithful*

---

4. A twin-chamber, covered conveyance mounted on a mule.
5. Nabíl-i 'Azam, *The Dawn-Breakers: Nabil's Narrative of the Early Days of the Bahá'í Revelation*, trans. and edited by Shoghi Effendi (Wilmette, Ill.: Bahá'í Publishing Trust, 1932) p. 298.

that when Táhirih was a guest in Bahá'u'lláh's summer home at Morgh Mahalleh in the foothills of the Alborz Mountains, north of Tehran, she would sit him (then a boy of five) on her lap and sing her odes in a beautiful voice.[6] She carried out a correspondence in verse (in rhymed couplets)—a common practice among Persian poets to this day—with Behjat, a Bábí poet in Shiraz. Some of that correspondence has survived.

However, while Táhirih was alive, there were no systematic efforts made to collect her verse—nor for some fifty years after her death would there be any such efforts made. The suppressed and precarious conditions under which the Bábís lived left no time for such attempts. The small number of poems, in any case, did not warrant the compilation of a customary *diván*.[7] Certainly, Táhirih herself, with her clear and urgent preoccupations, did not give any indication that she meant to make her imprint on history solely as a poet.

So far as can be determined now, Edward G. Browne, the renowned British orientalist, was the first person to acquire some of Táhirih's poems from Bábí, Azalí, and Bahá'í sources and to translate and publish them. It was, after all, the accounts of the desperate deeds and cruel martyrdoms of the early Bábís—Táhirih being unique and conspicuous among them—that had fired up Browne's romantic, rebellious, Byronic imagination in the first place and led him to search for these heroes, as chronicled in *A Year Amongst the Persians* in 1889-1890.[8]

---

6. For 'Abdu'l-Bahá's biographical sketch of Táhirih, see his *Memorials of the Faithful*, trans. and annotated by Marzieh Gail (Wilmette, Ill.: Bahá'í Publishing Trust, 1971) pp. 190-203.
7. The full canon of a poet's collected works.
8. Edward Granville Browne, *A Year Amongst the Persians* (London: Adam and Charles Black, 1893 and Cambridge: The University Press, 1927).

Amin Banani

In his tireless efforts to obtain primary sources for his monumental *Tarikh-i Zuhur al-Haqq*,[9] a history of the early Bábí era, Fazel Mazandarani acquired some previously uncirculated writings of Táhirih, including a few poems. In his volume, *Bábí and Bahá'í Poets of the First Century of the New Era*,[10] published in 1943, Bayza'i included a few samples of Táhirih's poems. Another Bahá'í author, Hesam Noqabá'i, also published a short essay about Táhirih in the 1970s, appending a few poems.[11] In 1944, in commemoration of the centenary of the Báb's declaration, the Azalí Bábís in Iran published anonymously a booklet entitled *Qurratu'l-'Ayn*,[12] which included a number of poems not cited in any of the previous publications.

However, by far the largest number of poems—53—is to be found in two undated manuscripts preserved in the National Archives of the Bahá'ís of Iran (now confiscated by the agents of the Islamic regime, and possibly destroyed), photocopies of which were made available to me. None of the above compendia, whether published or in manuscript form, provide any information about the genesis of their sources or the lines of their transmission. That there should be variant versions, copyist errors, and even possible attribution of works of other poets to

---

9. Fazel Mazandarani, Mirzá Asadollah, *Tarikh-i Zuhur al-Haqq*, Vol. 3 (Tehran: n.p., 1944).
10. Nematollah Bayza'i, *Tadhkirih-i Shu'aráy-i Qarn-i Avval-i Bahá'í* (Tehran: Bahá'í Publishing Trust, 1943 [1965-1970]).
11. Hesam Noqabá'i, *Táhirih: Qurratu'l-'Ayn* (Tehran: Bahá'í Publishing Committee, 1972).
12. *Bí-yád-i Sadumín Sal-í Shahádat-i Qurratu'l-'Ayn Nábighih-i Dawrán* (Tehran: n.p., 1944) <http://www.h-net.msu.edu/~bahai/areprint/tahirih/sadumin/sadumin.htm>.

Táhirih, or misappropriations of her poems by others is, therefore, to be expected. Controversies regarding authenticity cannot be avoided.

The Cultural and Historical Context

THE EBB AND FLOW OF LITERARY critical theories notwithstanding, the poems of Táhirih cannot be understood and appreciated outside their cultural and historical context. In the more than two and a half millennia of Persian cultural history, the impulse of renewal has been deeply encoded with spiritual yearning and religious fervor.[13] Nearly every movement of note and consequence, ranging in origin and motivation from profoundly sacred impulses to expressions of social and economic protest, and even urban or peasant uprisings, has appeared in the garb of a religious expectation or return. The worldview and the climate of thought of Persia is permeated by a religious outlook.

We read at the beginning of the poem "Lovers!":

ای عاشقان ای عاشقان شد آشکارا وجه حق
رفع حجب گردید ها ن از قدرت رب الخلق

خیزید کاین دم با بهاء ظاهر شود وجه خدا
بنگر به صد لطف وصفا آن روی روشن چون شفق

---

13. For the best treatment of this subject, see Alessandro Bausani, *Religion in Iran: From Zoroaster to Baha'ullah*, trans. by J. M. Marrchesi, distributed as volume eleven of the *Studies in the Bábí and Bahá'í Religions* series by Kalimát Press (New York: Bibliotheca Persica Press, 1959 ([2000]).

Amin Banani

یعنی ز خلاق زمان شد این جهان خرم چنان
روز قیام است ای مهان معدوم شد لیل غسق

آمد زمان راستی کژی شد اندر کاستی
آن شد که آن میخواستی از عدل و قانون و نسق

شد از میان جور وستم هنگام لطف است و کرم
ایدون به جای هر سقم شد جانشین قوت و رمق

Lovers! Creation veils his face no more!
Lovers, look! He himself is visible!

See! The face of God glows with glory:
Look, lovers! Bright, pure, blinding, beautiful!

Who made the cosmos turns earth green once more.
Rise! Rise from that dark so miserable!

The day of truth is here! Lies have turned to dust!
Order, justice, law are now possible.

Smashed, the despot's fist! God's hand opens:
grace pours down—not sorrow, pain, and trouble . . .

    Clearly, what these verses proclaim—leaving no room for ambiguity—is the rolling up of an old and decaying order replete with ignorance and injustice, and the coming of a new age of social and spiritual vigor. They signal the end of the era of expectations, the advent of the Promised One, the arrival of the Beloved. This code of renewal and resurrection—to come out of stagnation, to become young and fruitful again, to get over the past and to believe in the future, to uproot tyranny and to lay the foundation of justice, to end conflict and to spread love—is embedded in the myths of every human culture that has the stamina to survive and endure. It is a creative energy that manifests itself from time to time, causes great upheavals in society, shakes and frightens the worn-out established order, and opens up new horizons.

To approach Táhirih as a crucial figure in the unfolding movement of the Báb is the authentic view from within the texture of Shí'í Persian society at mid-nineteenth century. This is a movement that rapidly emerged from the matrix of convictions and expectations of the Shaykhí school of Shí'í Islam. Through the leadership of the Báb, the movement broke out of its Islamic cocoon with revolutionary energy, and under the guidance of Bahá'u'lláh it achieved its true radical potential and became a world religion.

So it is impossible to isolate Táhirih from the context of a religious movement. She was a leading actor in a grand passion of faith, a drama that at mid-nineteenth century occupied the center stage of the Persian world. The birth of a new religious movement from the roots of an established traditional faith is never calm and peaceful. Vehement denunciations, pronouncements of anathema, cries of heresy, torrents of outraged abuse and vilification, issued from the guardians of the old order, are to be expected. They are commonplace in the comparative history of all religions. From the outset of the Bábí movement in 1844, for a full hundred years, everything that was said or written in Persia about Táhirih (except for the adulatory and hagiographic accounts by the Bábís and Bahá'ís) was nothing but fanatical condemnations of an outraged orthodoxy. In the last half century, however, a new vogue of writing has come into being among Persian intellectuals based upon naïve application of borrowed analytical preconceptions to the events and personalities of their own society. They are primarily rooted in Marxian thought.

There is no denying the efficacy and the penetrating power of some Marxian analytical tools for the understanding of social history. The dialectic process and the importance of the notion of class are indispensable tools that a social historian can neglect only at the risk of impoverishment of the analysis. But a facile, unrigorous, and uncritical recourse to vulgar Marxism,[14] which has been discredited even in the Western, European societies from whose historical experience it was constructed, is doubly ludicrous when it is enforced upon the fabric of a Persian, Muslim society with a radically different set of dynamics. It leads to a gross distortion of the dynamics of social movements and a misreading of the motives of their prime movers.

In the heyday of the Stalinist era in 1938, M. S. Ivanov, a Russian historian in Moscow, published a short book called *Babidskoye Vastaniye v' Irana, 1848-1852* (Bábí Uprisings in Iran, 1848-1852). In it he subjected the Bábí movement, the personality and role of its founder, Sayyid 'Ali-Muhammad of Shiraz, and a number of his early followers—including Táhirih Qurratu'l-'Ayn—to a rudimentary, vulgar Marxist analysis. Shortly after that, the course of the Second World War led to partial occupation of Iran by Soviet troops and the rapid political rise of the Tudeh (Communist) Party with its massive appeal among the intelligentsia. It must be acknowledged that, from that time forward, nearly everything that has been written by

---

14. This term is not used in the popular pejorative sense here. Vulgar Marxism is actually a term coined by more careful Marxist thinkers to denote the simplistic, knee-jerk determinism of unsophisticated dogmatists.

this new group of intellectuals about the Bábí movement and the personality and historical role of Táhirih is traceable to Ivanov's book and its thought system. It is in principle a distorting approach.

The character of Táhirih, her mindset, her worldview, her motivations, and the depth of her passion cannot be examined detached from her deep faith in spiritual renewal, her eagerness to abrogate the Islamic law, and her willingness to sacrifice everything for the establishment of a new order. She must be viewed as she saw herself and within the framework of her own culture, if we are to appreciate the truly heroic dimensions of her life. No doubt there have been other women of sharp intellect, bold resolve, eloquent tongue, and charismatic power in Persian society who have felt the deep pain of tyrannical inequality. But seldom have the circumstances of their age allowed them to assert themselves and to leave an indelible mark upon history. The unique distinction of Táhirih is that she not only had all those qualities in superlatives, but that with all her natural gifts and innate abilities she set upon acquisition of knowledge and was quick to realize that knowledge is power.

She acquired the traditional learning of her culture, which was theology—with all its attendant disciplines of logic, rhetoric, and literature. In debates and disputes with turbaned patriarchs who looked upon religious learning as their monopoly, she outshone them all and henceforth was not willing to forgo the exercise of power that was the right of the learned. Throughout her short and adventurous life, she courageously fought for her own rights and those of other women and of all human beings. She never feared or wavered and, although she paid for her convictions with her life, she ultimately tri-

Amin Banani

umphed. The example that she has left for all struggling, justice-seeking, and liberating women—although in her native land it has been suppressed under covers of ignorance and prejudice—has not escaped the attention of outstanding men and women throughout the world.

In the second half of the nineteenth century, her name and feats of heroism were known among poets, artists, intellectuals, and progressive groups in Europe and North America. Her name was inscribed on the list of pioneers for emancipation of women in the first Congress for the Rights of Women held in America nearly a hundred years ago. Poems and homages were written to her in Italian, German, French, English, and Russian. Sarah Bernhardt, the best known French actress of her day, asked two of her contemporary authors, Catulle Mendes and Jule Bois, to write a play about Táhirih and the Bábís for her to portray on stage. The Russian poet Izabella Grinevskaya actually wrote such a play, which was staged at St. Petersburg.[15] It was after seeing this play and reading other accounts of Bábís and Bahá'ís that Leo Tolstoy became curious and sympathetic to the Bahá'í religion.[16]

Nor has all the attention and interest in Táhirih been confined to the Occident. Interest in and admiration for Táhirih have been remarkably persistent among the literary and intellectual Muslims of India and Pakistan, where dissertations, articles, and publications about her con-

---

15. See Jan T. Jasion, "Táhirih on the Russian Stage," in Sabir Afaqi, ed., *Táhirih in History: Perspectives from East and West*, Studies in the Bábí and Bahá'í Religions, Volume 16 (Los Angeles: Kalimát Press, 2004).
16. For early references to Táhirih and the Bábís and Bahá'ís in the West, see Moojan Momen, *The Bábí and Bahá'í Religions, 1844-1944: Some Contemporary Western Accounts* (Oxford: George Ronald, 1981).

tinue to proliferate.[17] Her story first appealed to the febrile, mercurial mind and creative talents of Muhammad Iqbal, the foremost Persian and Urdu poet of the subcontinent at the turn of the twentieth century. Ever since her surprise appearance as one of the three "martyr-guides" (the tenth-century Sufi mystic Hallaj, and the nineteenth-century Urdu poet Ghalib, are the other two) in Iqbal's *Javidnama*[18] (an account of the heavenly journey of the poet inspired by Dante's *Divine Comedy*), the fame and appeal of Táhirih among the Muslims of the subcontinent has been unflagging. In 1934, the Indian scholar Ishaque devoted a quarter of his book *Four Eminent Poetesses of Iran*[19] to Táhirih Qurratu'l-'Ayn, relying on poems gathered and published by Browne. Some of these same poems were published in Karachi in the appendix of Martha Root's *Táhirih the Pure* in 1938.[20]

Her Radical Vision

IN EVERY AGE, WHEN THE TEMPO of change and the pulse of social transformation is accelerated, the gravitational pull of the past and the resistance of the old order are also increased. A dynamic force is required to free any radical

---

17. For the impact of Táhirih on the Indo-Pakistan subcontinent, see Sabir Afaqi, "Qurratu'l-'Ayn in Urdu Literature" in *Táhirih in History* and idem., "Ta'thír-i Táhirih bar Shu'aráy-i Shibh-i Qárrih" (The influence of Táhirih on the poets of the subcontinent) in *Gulzár-i Shi'r va Adab* (Darmstadt, 1992).
18. Muhammad Iqbal, *Javidnama* (Lahore: n.p., 1932).
19. Mohammad Ishaque, "Qurratu'l-'Ayn: A Bábí Martyr," *Four Eminent Poetesses of Iran* (Calcutta: Iran Society, 1934 [1950]) pp. 28-35.
20. Martha L. Root, *Táhirih the Pure, Iran's Greatest Woman* (Karachi: n.p., 1938).

Amin Banani

movement for the new from the grip of the past and to thrust it into the new space. Táhirih was the most outstanding personification of this prodigious dynamic force.

At the outset of the Bábí movement, and especially after the incarceration and, finally, the execution of the Báb himself, it was not fully clear to the rapidly growing number of his followers what the advent of the "new age" meant. Even with his clear claim of being the return of the expected Qá'im (messiah) of Shí'í Islam, which was made at the midpoint of the short and tumultuous six years of his ministry (from his declaration in 1844 to his execution in 1850), the perceptions and expectations of most of his followers did not go beyond the idea of the literal fulfillment of Shí'í traditions and prophecies. They thought of the new movement as the means for the revival of Islam, not as an instrument for the abrogation of the Islamic law, freedom from its dogmas, and the dawn of a new dispensation and new order. Among the Bábís, it was Táhirih who was absolutely the most active, and eventually triumphant, exponent of a radical break with the past and a far-reaching progressive outlook.

Táhirih's role at the Conference of Badasht in 1848 was central to this drama. A number of Bábí leaders met fortuitously in the village of Badasht, in northeastern Persia, to discuss the future of the movement. Radicals argued with conservatives, and the conference appeared to be deadlocked. Táhirih's role was a masterpiece of combining signal with symbol, reality with drama, and secret code with open message. With one ploy she accomplished two feats. By removing her veil in the assemblage of men, she did at once proclaim—by word and by deed—both the abrogation of the law of Islam

A Woman for Our Time

and the emancipation and equality of women in the new Faith. That such a radical and momentous principle as the breaking of the old law and the advent of a new order was proclaimed by a woman, albeit confirmed and upheld by the Báb himself—as well as the fact that the first signal of the new order was an act which was clearly nothing less than an affirmation of emancipation and equality for rights for women—were not accidental. These two facets of Táhirih's dramatic and courageous act were mutually affirming and inseparable. Any attempt to focus on them separately or out of balance distorts the significance of Táhirih and obscures her true historical role.

Some historians have chosen to dwell on the substance of her doctrinal dissertations and dogmatic disputations and point to the absence of any explicit statement on the rights of women. They have concluded that she was nothing more than a heretically inclined theologian. Others have portrayed her as a fiery feminist pioneer, discounting her profound, spiritual motivation and her religiously integrated worldview. The statement attributed to her at the hour of her death: "You can kill me as soon as you like, but you cannot stop the emancipation of women,"[21] was probably never uttered—just as Louis XIV probably never said: "*L'etat c'est moi*" (I am the state). But both should have done so, for every act of their lives was a testament to the truth of those statements. Táhirih's indomitable will; her forthright claim to equal power based on learning; her implacable refusal to bow to domestic pressure; her painful choice to abandon home,

---

21. Root, *Táhirih the Pure*, p. 34.

Amin Banani

husband, and children rather than submit to injustice—and, above all, the dramatic gesture of public unveiling, these are all more eloquent than a thousand tracts on the rights of women. In the context of nineteenth-century Persian Shí'í society—or indeed even in the Iran of today—what more could a woman do that would mark her as a greater champion of women's rights?

Táhirih is indeed a heroine and pioneer model of emancipation, equality, and power of women because the Bábí movement prepared the ground for the inception of those struggles, and the Bahá'í Faith has carried them forward into our time. Both movements justify their progressive claims to uphold equality of rights for women as a fundamental tenet of their beliefs by making reference to Táhirih and her struggle.

The Context of the Poems

EXCEPT FOR HER VERSIFIED CORRESPONDENCE with Behjat, the Bábí poet of Shiraz, very little internal evidence can be deduced from the poems of Táhirih regarding the time, identity of the addressee, if any, or other specific circumstances surrounding their composition. Persian poetic traditions and practices being what they are, such ambiguities are not unusual. It is reasonable to assume that the one addressed or invoked by the poet's voice in some of the poems in this volume may be the Báb. Likewise, some may be directed toward Bahá'u'lláh, Quddus, or Subh-i Azal—other major Bábí figures of Táhirih's time. But any dogmatic insistence on such decoding is unwarranted.

It is safe to assume that the poems we have at hand were written in the last eight years of Táhirih's life. In the

A Woman for Our Time

last three years, she was captive in the house of Mahmúd Khán, the *kalántar* (mayor) of Tehran, and her contacts with her fellow Bábís were tenuous and haphazard. But her impact on the wife of the *kalántar*, and through her upon a large number of women of Tehran—especially the ladies of the upper classes and the royal court—was enormous. They were among the spreaders of her fame and reputation as a woman of tremendous eloquence.

It was through the devoted compliance of the wife of the *kalántar* that Táhirih's papers were entrusted to an unknown Bábí woman a few days after her death. Who was the woman who came for the papers? How had Táhirih prearranged for the posthumous disposition of those papers? Were there any poems among those papers? What became of those papers? Could any of the poems in our possession have come from that cache? These are tantalizing questions with answers shrouded in impenetrable darkness at this time.

"Point by Point"

FOR A HUNDRED AND FIFTY YEARS, despite a virtual blackout on public reference to Táhirih in her homeland, among the people of literary discernment wherever Persian poetry is known and appreciated, a mere mention of her name evokes first and foremost a ghazal with the opening line:

گر بتو افتدم نظر چهره بچهره رو برو

Gar be to oftadam nazar chehreh be chehreh roo be roo

If I met you face to face . . .

Amin Banani

It would not be an exaggeration to say that for a majority of people who have heard of Táhirih the poet, this is the only poem of hers they know. Seldom has a person's lasting credit as a memorable poet rested on a single work, as is the case here. It has been her signature poem, her calling card, and her ensign of identity. It evokes instant recognition of her. It is a ghazal of remarkable beauty, arresting imagery, passionate immediacy, rhythmic vitality, elegant rhetorical flourish, and artful musicality.

In the Persian poetic tradition—so long-lasting, so formal, so formulaic, with so many conventional rhetorical devices, and so much fixed and familiar imagery—individuality and originality can only be detected among the best poets. It is a variable complex of themes, vocabulary, tone, diction, and idiosyncratic devices that enable us to readily distinguish Hafez from Sa'di, and Sa'di from Rumi. As late as the mid-nineteenth century, the best of the meager number of poems we have of Táhirih have those marks of distinction, which make her poetic voice unique and readily recognizable. "Point by Point" has all the elements of her poetic personality stamped on it. It fits with the best of her poems as having come from the same bold, passionate pen.

It should come as no surprise then that the same relentless efforts that have striven from the moment of Táhirih's defiant emergence to suppress her voice, deny her existence, efface her memory, and erase every trace of her figure, would attempt to strike down her most recognizable banner of poetic identity. In the 1940s, at a time when various fresh assaults were being made against the origins, history, and integrity of the whole Bábí-Bahá'í movement, and crude forgeries were being produced to discredit its authenticity, a Persian scholar, Mohit

Tabátabá'i, known for his anti-Bahá'í animus from other contexts, published an article purporting to have discovered "Point by Point" in a manuscript copy of the collected poems of Tayer Isfahani, an obscure minor poet. Neither textological evidence nor literary arguments were presented for this claim. No information was given about the location of the discovery, the possible date of the manuscript, the name of the copyist, or the age of the paper. No competent scholar has attempted even one of these critical tasks. The purported *diván* containing this ghazal has, to the best of my knowledge, never been published.

With regard to all-important critical questions, no credible generic, stylistic evidence of kinship between this ghazal and the rest of the contents of Tayer Isfahani's *diván* is offered. Where are the other comparable poems from the person who could have produced such a masterwork? How can we discount a century-long identification of this poem with the intense, immediate, and unmistakable feminine voice of Táhirih, longing for her never-realized, face-to-face meeting with the Báb?

Under normal circumstances of free discourse and critical scholarship, all these questions should have been probed and answered. But in the land of Táhirih's birth, nothing like an open inquiry into anything related to the Bábí-Bahá'í movements has ever been permitted. A century and a half of relentless vilification and accusation has run its one-way course. Groundless repetition of misinformation has hardened into hatred, and ignorance has compounded into prejudice. Under this torrent of abuse, the Bábís and Bahá'ís have been denied the right to defend themselves. No civil open debate is ever permitted. Consequently, it is to be expected that a victim mentality, a submissive reaction, and a kind of ghetto-minded

Amin Banani

inwardness and isolation should sometimes be detected among the Bahá'ís of Iran. The mere unsupported claim of finding "Point by Point" in someone else's *díván*, as part of the all-pervasive assault on Táhirih and everything that she stood for, has resulted in the reflexive retreat of Hesam Noqabá'í, the Bahá'í biographer of Táhirih. Inexplicably, he accepted the claim of misattribution of the poem, rather than ask the relevant questions, challenge the claim, and put the burden of proof on the claimant.

As early as 1889, Edward Browne had observed the the reluctance of his Muslim sources to attribute poems to Táhirih, especially those that were widely admired. There was, even then, a desire on the part of learned Persians to assign the authorship of these poems to someone else. Only with the most diligent efforts could Browne locate even a few of Táhirih's verses. And he observes quite plainly:

> Although these poems . . . can only be referred very doubtfully to the authorship of Kurratu'l-'Ayn, it must be borne in mind that the odium which attaches to the name of Bábí amongst Persian Muhammadans would render impossible the recitation by them of verses confessedly composed by her. If, therefore, she were actually the authoress of poems, the grace and beauty of which compelled an involuntary admiration even from her enemies, it would seem extremely probable that they should seek to justify their right to admire them by attributing them to some other writer, and this view is supported by an assertion which I have heard made by a learned Persian with whom I was acquainted in Teherán, and who, though not actually a Bábí, did not lack a certain amount of sympathy for those who were such, to the effect that many poems written by Kurratu'l-'Ayn were amongst the favourite songs of the people, who were for

the most part unaware of their authorship. Open allusions to the Báb had, of course, been cut out or altered, so that no one could tell the source from whence they came.[22]

All this is not to insist that some feature of this ghazal's form—whether rhyme, choice of meter, or even possibly a whole line—may not have been echoed by Táhirih. We have noted above the importance of the time-honored practices of *esteqbál* and *tazmin* in the Persian literary tradition. Táhirih certainly made good use of these tools. Her ghazal "Lovers!" begin with a clear borrowing:

ای عاشقان ای عاشقان شد آشکارا وجه حق

Ey ásheqán, Ey ásheqán shod áshekárá vajh-e Haqq

Lovers! Creation veils his face no more!

which is an *esteqbal* of the famous ghazal of Rumi:

ای عاشقان ای عاشقان هنگام کوچ است از جهان

Ey ásheqán, Ey ásheqán hengám-e kooch ast az jahán

O lovers! O lovers, it's time to decamp from this world

The first line of her quintuplet *tarji'band* (a rondo of five-lined stanzas with a refrain) "From Those Locks":

---

22. Edward G. Browne, "The Bábís of Persia. II. Their Literature and Doctrines," *Journal of the Royal Asiatic Society* (London), Vol. 21 (1889) pp. 934-37

Amin Banani

ای به سر زلف تو سودای من

Ey be sar-e zolf-e to sowdá-ye man

From those dear locks must now my madness hang

is evocative of the famous *tarji'band* of the seventeenth-century poet, Hatef of Isfahan:

ای فدای تو هم دل و هم جان

Ey fadá-ye to ham del-o ham ján

O that I could sacrifice for you my heart and soul

"Running After You"

THE MYTHICAL IDENTIFICATION of one of Táhirih's poems with her rejection of a marriage proposal from the king, Nasiru'd-Dín Sháh (1831-1896), is questionable, but significant nevertheless.

After the conference of Badasht, Táhirih remained in hiding in northern Iran until she was arrested and brought to Tehran as a prisoner in January 1850. The Shah is supposed to have asked to see her, and she is supposed to have had a brief audience with him where she stood unveiled. We know that her husband had also been able to secure a meeting with the king, where he accused his wife of complicity in the murder of his father and demanded her execution. According to Edward G. Browne, Nasiru'd-Dín Sháh remarked, after seeing her: "I like her looks: leave her, and let her be."[23]

---

23. Idem., *A Traveller's Narrative written to illustrate the episode of the Báb* (Cambridge University Press, 1891; reprint: Amsterdam: Philo Press, 1975; reprint: Los Angeles: Kalimát Press, 2004) p. 313.

A Woman for Our Time

Therefore, she was placed under house arrest in Tehran in the home of the *kalántar*, where she remained for the rest of her life, until her martyrdom in 1852. As the story goes, shortly after her audience, the king sent her a letter (perhaps a poem, since he was known to dabble in poetry) proposing that if she would give up her Bábí religion and return to Islam, he would marry her and bring her into the royal harem as one of his wives.

Although this story appears in numerous accounts of Táhirih's life, it is difficult to locate its origin or find any way to vouch for its reliability. Nonetheless, there are certain elements that make the legend plausible. Nasiru'd-Dín Sháh would still have been a young man of nineteen years when this meeting took place. He had shown a curiosity in the Bábís and an interest in poetry during this period of his reign. Moreover, he had in just the previous year (1849) sought to reconcile a conflict between his government and his harem by ordering the marriage of his only full sister Malikzadih (then only thirteen years old) to his Prime Minister Amir Kabir.

So, it is perhaps not inconceivable that he may have sought to solve this Bábí problem with a proposal of marriage of his own. While this explanation cannot be offered as historical fact, it cannot be dismissed as impossible either. And so the story persists.

That such a small body of Táhirih's poetry, disseminated under such adverse conditions, should have gained such wide circulation and recognition—and acquired a mythical realm of associations—is in itself a sure sign of the magnetic and charismatic impact she made on all who came into her orbit.

Amin Banani

"Look Up!"

TÁHIRIH'S TRULY REVOLUTIONARY OUTLOOK and her clear vision of the new world that she struggled to bring about are revealed in a short poem of unusual power and forceful diction. It is the closest thing to a manifesto that can be found in all the literature of the Bábí movement. It is the first poem reproduced in this volume.

When Táhirih proclaims:

> Let warring ways be banished from the world
> Let Justice everywhere its carpet throw
>
> May Friendship ancient hatreds reconcile
> May love grow from the seed of love we sow!

we instantly recognize the acute and compassionate vision of a forward-looking woman who is painfully aware of the ancient hatreds that have been heaped upon her half of the human race. She sees her own emancipation in the liberation of the whole of humankind and seeks the remedy for ancient hatreds in friendship and love.

In terms of its meter, rhyme scheme, and length, this poem is a ghazal, a form of classical Persian love poem. However, this is as far from a traditional ghazal as one can get. There is nothing lyrical, nothing amatory, about it. It is a proclamation—epical, assertive, full of startling images and radical vocabulary that would not be encountered for another half century in Persia, until the post-Constitutional-Revolution poetry of men such as Farrokhi, Yazdi, and Lahuti.

A Woman for Our Time

In the original Persian, the abstract notion of a "guiding dawn" is depicted as an animate, awesome personification of nature that has begun to breathe. A sequence of deeply aspirated "h"s—*hán sobh-e hodá*—creates an aural affirmation of this remarkable animation. Its exalted rank is underlined by the use of the honorific verb *farmud*. The emphatic sibilant rhymes punctuate the triumphant and assertive statements.

Táhirih's open writ of dismissal handed to the clergy could not be more devastating. The unambiguous condemnation of cant and hypocrisy, of ignorance and superstition, and of fanaticism, all go to the root of what ailed her society. In its defiance of tyranny and cry for justice and equality, as well as its eloquent call for love and friendship, this poem bids well to be adopted as the anthem of Táhirih's heirs.

"Just Let the Wind . . ."

NO POEM OF TÁHIRIH is more emphatic, more revealing in its beautiful imagery of feminine charm and allure, more audacious in its self-assurance than the lines of this short poem we have titled "Just Let the Wind . . ." Here we find ourselves back in the tonal, metaphoric, and image world of classical Persian verse, with its familiar tropes and strong, musical vowels.

The "wild gazelle" (*áhuván-e sahrá*), the "flashing eyes" painted with black (*narges-e shahlá*), and "golden looking-glass" (*á'ine-ye motallá*) create a landscape of known terrain. But it is inhabited by a woman of irrepressible passion, indomitable will, and awesome power.

Amin Banani

    Táhirih's power here admits to no limits: she proclaims that her feminine beauty and attraction will overpower, not only the whole world, but the heavens too. In the third breathtaking couplet of the poem, Táhirih imagines the sun itself as only a mirror that reflects the dazzle of her face each dawn.

    This is not a face that could be hidden by a veil, and this is not a voice that could be choked into silence.

On Translating a Persian Mystical Poet

by Jascha Kessler

A RELIGIOUS TEXT confronts the translator with an ineluctable obstacle, one that to the skeptic's mind may seem insuperable: it is usually poetry, the very utterance of which is a mystery, and an enigma. No sooner is it voiced, than it at once enters time and eternity both; no sooner is it locked in the unreachable past, than its sustaining waters pour from the rock of death and nothingness. What else of human making, what else in human experience, is like that? It is the paradox of poetry that it persists through ages, yet is known only in the present; it is read by the living. And to read is to interpret; in short, to translate.

The past, it has been said, is a foreign country. It cannot be entered. Its relics can however be brought out. That is the reason why new translations are attempted. They are needed especially in a world like ours, where diverse peoples—however distant, however alien their societies or cultures may be from one another—are nonetheless contiguous in time. Today a telephone call, a radio or television broadcast connects them. By means of ubiquitous and omnipresent media, they are virtual to one another. Physical distance itself is inconsiderable, because no place on the globe is much more than a day's flying-time from any other.

Such propinquity is also riddled with complexity. Our planet is populated by many societies that, from the Western perspective, present cultural universes historically so remote from our own that they seem as distant as those we think of as belonging to centuries long past. These various "times past" live irreducibly *present* to us. In other words, the peoples who occupy different portions of the shrunken space to which our planet is now reduced remain psychologically distant from one another, and their differences can indeed be vast.

This situation creates the problem that translation faces and exemplifies. A tourist, for instance, flies over India at 35,000 feet, while contemplating in a glossy airline magazine the photograph of a naked *sadhu* descending a ghat to perform an ablution in the Ganges. How may either of these begin to comprehend the other's world? They exist in a novel, intimate proximity; at the same time, aside from the immanent problem of contagious contact, they are in no way near one another!

Given such a consideration, how can any meaningful communication occur? How can we grasp the experience of people who have not yet entered our history? And how should they themselves apprehend ours? Perhaps it is not possible. One notices it particularly and poignantly in the case of major religious beliefs and traditional practices that have their origins in ancient times, but which persist today opaque to others, syncretic and eclectic rituals that have appeared in the West notwithstanding. In any case, a poetry embodying the values of a culture that has not changed as rapidly as ours in the West will bring up a formidable challenge to translation. Even though the English or the French and the Egyptians may play and even adapt our pop and rock music, and watch our dubbed movies and television shows, it scarcely signifies identification. The transfer to Asia or Africa of Western technology is seldom, if ever, accompanied by any baggage of understanding of its intrinsic historical development, or its immanent cultural value. Whereas technology may be quite culturally neutral, it may well be culturally *neuter* as well. In North America, Native Americans took to the back of the Spanish horse about 500 years ago, and later adopted the rifle; yet today they remain stubbornly "Indian," insofar as they have managed to survive. And one need merely cite the savage, outright warfare obtaining in many parts of the globe today, where the cultures of Europe and North America (that is, the historical works and creations of the West) are in collision with those of the Middle East, India, and the Far East. Any traveler, even a casual tourist, is aware of that from the first step on alien ground.

Since any language entrains its cultural history, if it endures, so does its philosophy, its mythology and theology. These remain to be read in its literature, whether or not even its own contemporary speakers are able to take ancient, traditional significance from its words. What persists best and says the most is usually to be found in poetry, that heavily-condensed speech that contains the essence of experience as it was fixed by emotion and thought, words images set in sentences that impress themselves upon the mind. This may be so because the

Jascha Kessler

archaic and traditional are permeated—and saturated—with poetry. The images and forms of material objects of art also have such power; but words carry speakable thoughts, the formulated abstractions of ideas immanent in a culture. Expressive as other arts may be, they cannot *explain* themselves, while language does precisely that.

Explanation is a process inherent also in the act of translation. In the case of a poet like Táhirih, one must at the outset resolve a practical dilemma: whether to offer her in contemporary American poetry in the current mode of loose, arbitrary, prosaic "free" verse, nowadays a collage of decayed modernist practice, or attempt to reproduce the verse forms she herself employed, forms moreover not part of the English, not to mention the European, tradition. The products of the easy first choice would result in slack paraphrase, sufficient perhaps for a reader who wishes merely to approach what she says. A prose or prosaic rendering will take care of that. But, when Táhirih wrote theology, she wrote prose, not verse.

The second choice offers yet another dilemma: to replicate her poems in their original forms necessitates either the kind of archaizing common among nineteenth-century translators of Sanskrit, Persian, and Arabic—an anachronism interdicted by the best of our twentieth-century practitioners from Ezra Pound on down—or the adoption of loose facsimiles of her strict forms. Loose, because our usage and our sensibility is no longer equipped for the rhyming patterns the Persian language affords. We cannot tolerate very much in the way of inverted, contorted, "poetical" syntax; and in English we have too few rhymes to employ, especially identical rhymes, in serious, often exalted, verse. One can offer to reproduce Persian measures; but rocking or rolling meter,

Translating a Persian Mystic Poet

the anapæstic foot in particular, rather lend themselves to light or satiric verse in our language—or else to the lofty, as it was employed in the bardic manner of William Blake, or the hortatory, incantatory Walt Whitman, or Robinson Jeffers in the mid-twentieth century. Táhirih's poems, however, are lyric in scale, concentrated in statement, and intense in tone. Any attempt to render them (pseudo-)epical would have required inflation, supererogatory locutions, images, phrases—resulting in crib-like explanation and inevitable bowdlerization.

My solution was to follow her rhymed verses, trying for more or less a similar number of words, so as to carry the denotational freight of each sentence, but to set them down in our common measure, iambic pentameter. The results are perhaps not *complete* translation, were such a thing possible: that is, the poems are not said out as they would be were Táhirih herself writing them in America today, were such a thing conceivable. (I don't think it *is* properly conceivable, however, since in the chronicle of earthly existence, each of us is fated to reside *only* in our own time and place.)

I have always tried to render the speech of those contemporary poets I have translated from the Hungarian, Bulgarian, Italian, Slovak, Finnish, or Persian by what I fancy they *might* sound like in our present lingo, speaking American. For example, in *Bride of Acacias*, Amin Banani's and my translation from the Persian of the poetry of Forugh Farrokhzad (1934-1967), the fact that the poet's mature work was almost entirely written in free verse made for an idiomatic, fluent American speech that replicated her lines. Of course, Forugh's psychology, being "modern," and her values Western, it was not too hard to enter her universe or identify with her spirit, as it were, so as to "hear" her voice.

Jascha Kessler

Táhirih is quite another matter. Mystical, ecstatic poetry, devotional and visionary by turn, is what most of this selection consists of. Although her imagery and symbolism may be conventional to her time and place, it can scarcely seem familiar to English-speaking readers. I surmise that it will certainly also appear somewhat exotic, perhaps puzzling, to contemporary Persian speakers, given the disruptions of the twentieth century, and given as well her condemnation and murder by the orthodox of Islam in 1852. What is important, indeed crucial, in reading Táhirih, it seems to me, is the retention of the succinct, symbolic imagery based on her religious tradition, and derived from Persia's greatest poets. *That* is what cannot be "translated," for it remains always where she found it, and as she set it in her poems. It may nevertheless be "repeated" by means of what can be taken for its reasonable facsimiles in our language and, with the help and guidance of commentary, rendered familiar enough to be experienced by a sympathetic reader.

My decision was therefore to carry her over into our vernacular in both form and content, deliberately risking an exotic, sometimes anachronistic, effect. I see nothing to be gained by removing her altogether from the forms of her nineteenth-century Persian world, which most assuredly would have occurred in any free-verse translation. Táhirih, it should be remembered, was first and foremost writing *poems*. She was writing song, meditation, prayer, exordium, ecstatic outpouring—in *formal* verses. In short, she crafted her utterance. And that is why I have tried to show her as a poet, not as the purveyor of a passionate and esoteric religiosity, although the work obviously and naturally contains material wholly expressive of just that.

Translating a Persian Mystic Poet

If the reader can believe that it is Táhirih who is speaking in these poems, Táhirih as she stands in the Persian, then I have succeeded in my aim to represent her—again, as *she* is, and not as she would look garbed in the casual American dress of fashion today. Underlying my judgment that in practice this was the best course to follow lies a premise I hope is shared by my collaborator, Amin Banani, who proposed the project and prepared the texts for me, as well as by those of Táhirih's co-religionists unable to read her work except in this Englishing. The premise cannot be over-emphasized: Her poetry remains rooted absolutely in her time and place—and her tradition. She is seen best by her own light.

So, let us take the risk of exhibiting her in the costume of the forms she employed, so that we may read and admire and come to understand her rather more as she was, and somewhat less as we might see her in our time. In that way we shall perhaps be able to accept my simulacra of the verses in which she expressed herself. Here they stand as somewhat exotic (i.e., curious, though not, I think, quaint) English poems. Let us read her in much the same manner as we read the poetry of our seventeenth-century English mystics and ecstatics, Herbert, Vaughan, Traherne, and Crashaw. Such a premise includes the assumption I put forward earlier: that poetry is both as fugitive as our time on earth and as transcendental as language itself seems to be. If in these versions I have succeeded to some small extent in recomposing her for us today, then the reader will have some useful notion of who and what Táhirih in her exalted moments was—those moments caught, and perhaps forever held, in the words of her poems.

Jascha Kessler

To satisfy the reader's possible curiosity about our working method, it may be practical to add here simply that the lines of her poems were marked for me by Amin Banani as to meter, and set down in Persian written in the Roman alphabet. The lines were paralleled through metaphrase into English lines, that is, they followed the original word order and syntax. The act of "translating" the Persian takes place in the next step, in which I seek to paraphrase those texts into what is, I hope, poetry in our language.

Editor's Note

IN THIS VOLUME, the poems of Qurratu'l-'Ayn, Táhirih, have not been translated word for word into English. Such a translation would, of course, result in nonsense, or at best, in an awkward and wooden rendering of verses that are, in their original languages, flowing, startling, and evocative. Instead, we have attempted to produce translations that are poems in their own right, English poems that capture at least some of the fire and emotion of the originals.

What is poetry, after all? It is the language that we turn to when there is no language that can express our thoughts and feelings. Poetry is, in fact, the attempt to move beyond language, to communicate states of mind and states of spirit that cannot be communicated in words, but which nonetheless must be expressed. A poem cannot capture an emotion or a spiritual state: it can only suggest, or better, evoke, such a state. If it doesn't, then the poem is a failure.

On the face of it then, the attempt to translate a poem into another language would seem impossible. Even if we were to take a poem in English and substitute different English words for similar words in the original, we would destroy the poem and ruin its beauty. How can all the words of a poem be changed for words in a different lan-

Editor's Note

guage, with their foreign connotations and associations, and preserve anything of the original?

Yet, as Jascha Kessler points out in his essay, the attempt must be made. And we find that it is possible. The spirit at least of a poem can be translated, if not the exact words.

To give the reader an idea of the process of translation that all of the poems here were subjected to, we have provided below: the original Persian of "Just Let the Wind . . ."; a transliteration of the Persian (to provide an idea of sound and meter); a word-for-word literal translation; and the English poem as it was finally rendered. In the notes at the end of the book, we have provided a number of literal translations of specific lines or stanzas for various poems (see pp. 109-145).

PERSIAN POEM:

اگر باد دهـــم ژلف عنبر آسا را
اسیر خویش کنم آهوان صحـــرا را
و گر به نرگس شهلای خویش نرمه کشم
بروز تیـــره نشانم تمام دنیا را
بـــرائ دیدن رویم سپهر هردم صبح
برون برآورد آئینــــــه مطلّا را
گذار من بکلیسا اگر فتـــد روزی
بدین خویش برم دخـــــتران ترسا را

Editor's Note

TRANSLITERATION:

> Agar be bád daham zolf-e anbar ásá rá
> Aseer-e khish konam áhuán-e sahrá rá
> Vagar be nargas-e shahlá-ye khish sormeh kesham
> Be rooz-e teereh neshánam tamám-e donyá rá
> Baráye didan-e rooyam sepehr har dam sobh
> Boroon bar ávarad áyine-ye motallá rá
> Gozár-e man be kelisá agar fetad roozi
> Be deen-e khish baram dokhtarán-e tarsá rá

LITERAL TRANSLATION:

> if / to / wind / I give / hair of / amber / scent
> captive of / mine / I would make / deer of / wilderness
> if / to / narcissus (eyes) / blue-black / mine / collyrium / I would draw
> to / day of / dark / I would set / entire / world
> for / seeing / my face / sphere / every / early / morning
> outside / brings out / mirror of / gilt
> path / mine / by / church / if / should fall / one day
> to / religion / mine / I would take / girls of / piety

THE ENGLISH POEM:

Just Let the Wind . . .

Just let the wind untie my perfumed hair,
my net would capture every wild gazelle.

Just let me paint my flashing eyes with black,
and I would turn the day as dark as hell.

Yearning, each dawn, to see my dazzling face,
the heaven lifts its golden looking-glass.

If I should pass a church by chance today,
Christ's own virgins would rush to my gospel.

Editor's Note

THE TRANSLITERATION of Persian and Arabic words, phrases, and names found in this book is not completely consistent. Unfortunately, there is no one system of transliteration that is used universally, and so various systems compete. For example, the name:

طاهره

may be variously rendered into Latin letters as: Ṭáhirih, Táhirih, Tahereh, Tahira, etc. And these are by no means all of the choices. The publisher's house style produces: Táhirih, the form that is used in this book. But, it has the unfortunate consequence of distorting the correct pronunciation of the name (pronounced Ta-he-*reh*) in English.

We have departed from our house style, therefore, when attempting to convey the sounds of Persian or Arabic (which are, of course, different languages) or when a more phonetic spelling seemed appropriate. This has resulted in inevitable inconsistencies, for which we apologize.

THE POEMS are printed in this volume both in English and in their original languages. Since Persian and Arabic are read from right to left, the original Persian *precedes* the English (on shaded pages). For longer poems, the first page of the Persian/Arabic poem faces the first page of the English, and the texts are read in opposite directions.

A FURTHER WARNING must be offered the careful bilingual reader of this volume concerning the calligraphic Persian texts. In a very few instances, there are variances in the

Editor's Note

number of lines, as well as in the component words, of a given poem between the Persian and the English texts. As has been noted in the introduction, the possibility of a definitive critical text of Táhirih's poems is out of the question at this time. Our translations were made from the oldest manuscripts and printed sources available. For aesthetic reasons, the *nasta'liq* calligraphy received from Pakistan was used instead of the mechanical *naskh* of the word processor, despite its small number of variants from the translations. These variants, as well as missing or extra lines, order of the lines, and other minor errors are indicated in the notes.

WE ARE GRATEFUL to Rasheed Butt (Pakistan) and to Iraj Mahingostar (United States) for providing the masterful calligraphy of the poems in *nasta'liq* script.

The Poems

هان صبح هدی افسر مود آغاز تنفس !
روشن همه عالم شد ز آفاق و زانفس

دیگر ننشیند شیخ بر مسندِ تزویر
دیگر نه شود مسجد دُکانِ تقدّس

ببریده شود رشتهٔ تحت الحنکِ ازم
نه شیخ بجا ماند، نه زرق و تدلّس

آزاد شود دهر ز اوهام و خرافات
آسوده شود خلق ز تخییل و توسوس

محکوم شود ظلم ببازوئی مساوات
معدوم شود جهل ز نیروے تفرّس

گسترده شود در همه جا فرشِ عدالت
افشانده شود در همه جا تخمِ توّنس

مرفوع شود حکم خلاف از همه آفاق
تبدیل شود اصلِ تباین بتجانس

هان صبح بدی دمد و آغاز تنفس !

Look Up!

Look up! Our dawning day draws its first breath!
The world grows light! Our souls begin to glow!

No ranting shaykh rules from his pulpit throne
No mosque hawks holiness it does not know

No sham, no pious fraud, no priest commands!
The turban's knot cut to its root below!

No more conjurations! No spells! No ghosts!
Good riddance! We are done with folly's show!

The search for Truth shall drive out ignorance
Equality shall strike the despots low

Let warring ways be banished from the world
Let Justice everywhere its carpet throw

May Friendship ancient hatreds reconcile
May love grow from the seed of love we sow!

اگر باد دهـم زلف عنبر آسا را
اسیر خویش کنم آهوان صحرا را

وگر به نرگس شهلای خویش سرمه کشم
بروز تیره نشانم تمام دنیا را

برائے دیدن رویم سپهر هر دم صبح
برون برآورد آئینهٔ مطلّا را

گذار من بکلیسا اگر فتد روزی
بدین خویش برم دختران ترسا را

اگر بگذارد و هم زلفت عبیر آسا را

Just Let the Wind . . .

Just let the wind untie my perfumed hair,
my net would capture every wild gazelle.

Just let me paint my flashing eyes with black,
and I would turn the day as dark as hell.

Yearning, each dawn, to see my dazzling face,
the heaven lifts its golden looking-glass.

If I should pass a church by chance today,
Christ's own virgins would rush to my gospel.

آمد او با جلوه‌های سرمدی
ظاهر او بنمود وجه احدی
لیک غافل جملهٔ ارباب هوش
از تفرد های جذبای سروش
احمد است اینکه نزیل آمد نزیل
از سما عزم به آیات جلیل

عالمی را از شرر پرشور کرد
آدمی را او سراسر نور کرد
طاهره بردار پرده از میان
تا بیاید بترخیبی در عیان
گوی اَحمَدُ هُوَ رَتبِ جَمیل
قَد تَفَشَّعَ مِن طرازاتِ الجلیل

He Has Come!

He's come! He's here to tear our veils away
He's here! He's come to show us God today

Yet masters of the mind refuse to hear
and heaven's song is wasted on their ear

He's come to bring us life beyond all praise
He lights this world: his voice is heaven's blaze

Its fire burns our world with wild delight
Stripped bare we stand: we're made of purest light!

Lift the veil, Táhirih! He's now exposed!
His hidden mystery has been disclosed!

And say: The Lord in glowing clothes is dressed!
Praised be his beauty, and forever blessed!

هان که امر مُبرمم ظاهر شده
حکم محکم آیهٔ قاهر شده

برکن اَلباس حدود و پس قیود
خویش را انداز در دریای جود

تا به کی در عالم پُرشور و شر
دور هستی تو ز مقصد دور، دور

امر ما ظاهر شده از کاف و نون
گو مِن الله اِلیهِ راجعون

آن که امر مبرمم ظاهر شده

Proclamation

Hear this! My one and only Cause is true.
The words I speak mean victory for you.

Off with rags of law and pious fashion!
Swim naked in the sea of compassion!

How long will you drift through this world of war,
far from the safety of your native shore?

Sing, Be! Our Cause stands strong, both clear and plain:
"What comes from God returns to God again!"

چو ظهور آن شه ما عروف عظمت شئون جلاله

بجهان جان شد از شرف حضرت دعوت مقاله

همه جان جملهٔ انس و جان شد در قدوم وی ارمغان

به تعشّق آمده عاشقان قبَل سبیل وصاله

طلع البهاء و شرقت فرق ظهر البهاء و اللّمعة

قلل الوجود نضیرة فلکاً لوجه جماله

همه آیه‌های مسلسله زلسان او شده نازله

همه انبیاء همه وله متبرّجاً بجماله

The King Walked In

The King walked in, and no one saw him come.
His words, how beautiful! His face, how fair!

Now, everyone will perish at his feet.
His lovers, drunk on joy, run to be there.

The sun of Glory risen high! Glory!
it shines now—sparkling, glowing in the air.

The mountain peaks bow low before his beauty.
They circle 'round like pilgrims lost in prayer.

And endless verses flow from his sweet tongue.
Prophets of old rush from the past to hear.

بتموّج آمده آن کمی که بحر بلاش بحر تمّی

منتظر است بهر وی دو هـــزار وادی کربلا

ز کمان آن رُخ پر دله ز کمند آن مه ده دله

دو هزار فـــرقه و سلسله متفرقـــاً متسلسلا

همه موسیـان عمائیش همـــه عیسیـان بهائیش

همه دلبران بعث تائیش متولّهـــاً متنزِّلا

بحر الوجود تموّجت یعــــل الشّهود تولّجت

شفق الخمود تلجلجت بلغـــت همجمــــلا

هکل جبـــال زطلعتش، قلل جبال زرفعتش

دول جلال ز سطوتش متخشعاً متـــــزلزلا

دلم از دو زلف سیاه او و ز فــــراق روی چو ماه او

به تراب مقــــدم راه او شده خون من متبلبلا

زعم توایّ مه مهربان ز فراقت آشفته دلبران

شد روح هیکل جسمیان متفقــاً متنخّلا

تو آن تشعشع روی خود تو آن ملتمع موی خود

که رسانیم تو به کوی خـــود متفــــرّعــــاً متجلّی

هله اے گروه عمائیان بکشید هلهله ولا
که ظهور دلبر ما عیان شد فاش و ظاهر بر ملا
برنید نغمه ز هر طرف که ز وجه طلعت معروف
رفع الغطاء وقت کشف ظلم اللیال قد انجلی
برسید با سپه طرب صنمی مجسم صمدی عرب
بدمید شمس ز ما غرب بدو ید الله مهرولا
فوران نار ز ارض فاء نوران نور ز مشهر طاء
ظهر ان روح ز شطرها و لقد علا و قد اعتلا
طیر بعماء تکفکفت ورق البهاء تصفصفت
دیک الضیاء تذ ورقت مسجم لاتجلّلا
ز ظهور آن شه آلهه زالست آن مه مالهه
شده آلهه همه الهه تبغّیات بلی بلی

هله هلے گروہ عمائیاں بکشید هله هله ڑ ولا

Start Shouting!

Angels! Saints! All you holy ones above!
My true lover just walked in. Start shouting!

Night turned to day, dark into light. He's here
without a veil to hide his face. Start singing!

The Sun is up, it's rising in the West.
You armies of God's ecstasy! Start moving!

Fars is set aflame, and Tehran's burning.
Pure spirit rises from his place. Start dancing!

At daybreak nightingales don't sing. The cock
struts out and birds of Glory start praising.

When my lover asks, *Am I not your Lord?*
even the gods reply in awe, *Thou art.*

His mighty river overflows, and floods
a thousand desert Karbalas—to start.

The arches of his eyes will make the feuds
of warring faiths and creeds to disappear.

Moses and Jesus in heaven are stunned,
and all the holy ones are lost down here.

Two thousand Muhammads hear thunderbolts,
they wrap themselves in cloaks, tremble in fear.

The sea storms—it casts up its shining pearls.
To give way to the sun, the dawn makes haste.

Men melt, mountains quake before his beauty.
His majesty lays whole kingdoms to waste.

And me, destroyed by two strands of his hair.
The moon of his face drives me to despair.

Beloved, when will I see you up there,
see the light of your face, the shine of your hair?

The moon now has me mad with restless love
in the agony of my separation.

ای صبا بگو از من آن عزیز بهائی را
اینچنین روا باشد طلعت بهائی را

ابر لطف آن محبوب رشحه رشحه میبارد
بر هبیا کل مطروح محو سِتر هائی را

نسمهٔ عراقیش میوزد بسی روحا
زنده می نماید او بهیکل سوائی را

باب را بکن غرّه بیش شد مفتح ابواب
لطف او شده سائل اهل فتح طائی را

با بهیان نوریه جنبگی برون آئید
از حجاب بهائی عزّ بنگر ید فائی را

طلعت مبین ناگه طالع از حجاب عزّ
مشنو ای عزیز من نطق من ترائی را

ای صبا بگو از من آن عـــزیز ئی را

Morning Breezes

Morning breezes, take my supplication,
to the kingdom of Bahá, no other place—

where only rain can wash clean the corpses
of those struck dead when they behold his face,

where winds of mercy blow in from Iraq
to raise the fallen back to life reborn.

The Western Gate has unlocked all the gates,
with bounties from the city of Tehran.

You Bábís from the province of pure Light!
Strip off your splendid veils, just look and see.

Believers, he has thrown away his veil,
so forget the verse "You will never behold me."

مهر تو را دل حـــزین بافته بر قماش جان
رشته به رشته رنخ به نخ تار به تار پو به پو
در دل خویش طاهره گشت و ندید جز تو را
صفحه به صفحه لا به لا پرده به پرده تو به تو

گر بتو افتدم نظر چهره بچهره رو برو
شرح دهم غم تو را آنکه به نکته مو بمو

از پی دیدن رخت همچو صبا فتاده‌ام
خانه بخانه در بدر کوچه به کوچه کو بکو

میرود از فراق تو خون دل از دو دیده‌ام
دجله بدجله یم به یم چشمه به چشمه جو بجو

دور دهان تنگ تو عارض عنبرین خطت
غنچه به غنچه گل به گل لاله به لاله بو به بو

ابرو و چشم و خال تو صید نموده مرغ دل
طبع بطبع دل بدل مهر بمهر خو به خو

گر تو افتد بہ نظر چہرہ بچسمۂ رو برو

Point by Point

If I met you face to face, I
would retrace—erase!—my heartbreak,
pain by pain,
ache by ache,
word by word,
point by point.

In search of you—just your face!—I
roam through the streets lost in disgrace,
house to house,
lane to lane,
place to place,
door to door.

My heart hopeless—broken, crushed!—I
heard it pound, till blood gushed from me,
fountain by fountain,
stream by stream,
river by river,
sea by sea.

The garden of your lips—your cheeks!—
your perfumed hair, I wander there,
bloom to bloom,
rose to rose,
petal to petal,
scent to scent.

Your eyebrow—your eye!—and the mole
on your face, somehow they tie me,
trait to trait,
kindness to kindness,
passion to passion,
love to love.

While I grieve, with love—your love!—I
will reweave the fabric of my soul,
stitch by stitch,
thread by thread,
warp by warp,
woof by woof.

Last, I—Táhirih—searched my heart, I
looked line by line. What did I find?
You and you,
you and you,
you and you.

لمعات وجهک اشرقت و شعاع طلعتک اعتلی

ز چه رو الست بر نجم زنی بزن که بلی بلی

بجواب سبیل الست تو ز و لا چو کوس بلا زدم

همه خیمه زد بدر دلم سپه غنم و چشم بلا

من و عشق آن مه خوبرو که چو زد صلای بلا بر او

به نشاط و قهقهه شد فرو که انا الشهید به کربلا

چو شنید ناله مرگ من پی ساز من شد برگ من

فمشی الی مهدولا و بکی علی مجل جلا

چه شود که آتش حسرتی ز نیم بضعة طور دل

فشکسته و دگشته متدکداً متنزلا

پی خوان دعوت عشق او همه شب ز خیل گرو بیان

رسد این صفیر هی همینی که گروه غم زده الصلا

تو که فلس ماهی حیرتی چه زنی ز بحر وجود دم

بنشین چو طاهره دمبدم بشنو فروش ترنگ لا

Your Brilliant Face

When the burning sun of your face first dawned,
you dazed me by your light at my day's start.

So speak the words: *"Am I not your Lord?"*
My heartbeat will reply: *"Thou art. Thou art."*

You asked: *"Am I not?"* I said: *"Yes, Thou art."*
Then disaster set up camp inside my heart.

Alone I gaze at the moon of your face:
When slain at Karbalá you danced and leapt,

but when you heard them wailing for my death,
you grabbed my things, rushed to my side, and wept.

You raised me up high, then tore me to rubble.
So light a spark now—set the trash afire.

I hear angels in ceaseless song: *"Sad lovers!
Come join his feast: Eat all that you desire."*

Be still, with Táhirih. Will you hold back the sea?
Hear Leviathan roar: *"There is no God but Me."*

خال بکنج لب یکی طرّهٔ مشک فام دو
دلئے بحال مرغ دل دانه یکے و دام دو

محتسب است و شیخ و من صحبت عشق در میان
از چه کنم مجابشان پخته یکی و خام دو

از رخ و زلف آن صنم از من است آه همچو شب
وائے بروزگار من روز یکے و شام دو

ساقی ماه هدی من از چه نشسته غافلی
باده بیار می بده نقد یکی و دام دو

مست دو چشم دلربا همچو قتراب پر نمے
در کف ترک مست بین باده یکی و جام دو

کشتهٔ تیغ ابرویت گشته هزار همچو من
بستهٔ چشم جادویت میم سی یکے و لام دو

وعده وصل میدهی لیک وفا نمی کنی
من بجهان ندیده ام مرد و یے یکے و کام دو

گاه بجوان سگ ِ درت گاه کمینه چاکرت
فرق نمی کند مرا بنده یکے و نام دو

A Beauty Mark

That mole on your lip, those two curls above:
One seed, two springs—and my poor heart is snared!

A priest, a judge, and I—we talk of love,
but what is there that I can teach two fools?

Your face, your curls, turn day to night, my dove:
One day that is night—two nights in a day?

The grape-vat swells with the vintner's child of
the vine. The bastard—one dad, and two moms!

Cupbearer! Where's our wine? Up, Moonface! Move!
Bill them for two—I'll pay for mine in cash!

Two eyes, and I'm drunk: I've lost my heart's trove:
lost in the Turk's two cups—yet why one wine?

Your eyebrows' sword slew thousands, then you drove
whole nations mad—like me—just with your eyes!

You broke your promise, the union of love!
Can any man who swears two vows be good?

Call me your watchdog, but still I won't move.
I am your servant: one slave with two names!

در رهِ عشقت ای صنم شیفتهٔ بلامنم
چند مغایرت کنی با غمت آشنا منم

پرده بروی بسته‌ئی زلف بهم شکسته‌ئی
از همه خلق رسته‌ئی از همگان جدا منم

شیر توئی شکر توئی شاخه توئی ثمر توئی
شمس توئی قمر توئی ذره منم هما منم

نخل توئی رطب توئی لعبت نوش لب توئی
خواجهٔ با ادب توئی بندهٔ بی حیا منم

کعبه توئی صنم توئی دیر توئی حرم توئی
دلبر محترم توئی عاشق بی نوا منم

من زیم تو نیم هم نی زکم و ز بیش هم
چون بتو متصل شدم بی حد و انتها منم

شاهد شوخ دلبرا گفت بسوی من بیا
رسته ز کبر و از ریا مظهر کبریا منم

طاهره خاکپای توست می لقای تو
منتظر عطائ تو معترف خطا منم

In Pursuit

In pursuit of your love, my idol, mad for disaster am I.
But you will not desert me, so immersed in your sorrows am I.

You veiled your face, tortured the locks of your hair. You
threw them all behind you—but not me. Here am I.

You are milk and nectar, you are the tree and its fruit. You
are the sun and the moon—an atom, just a speck am I.

You are palm and date, you are my honey-lipped beauty. You
are the perfect master, and just a shameless slave am I.

You are my Ka'aba, my idol, my shrine and altar. You
are high, rich, and mighty—a helpless lover here am I.

But half a drop in your ocean am I, and merged in you,
no more, no less—now infinite, eternal here am I.

My playful lover stole my heart. He said: You come to me!
Now, modest and manifest magnificence here am I.

Táhirih, in the dust, and drunk on the one face I see:
Alone I await your blessing: a sinner here am I.

سجود و جهنگ فرضاً علی نے الصلواتی
ترا پرستم اگر فی المثل جو لات و مناتی
بچشم خویش نظر کن مرا مگو ز چه مستی
در آئینهٔ رخ خود بین مرا مپرس ز چه ماتی
نرفته در عتبات زهی رخ کعبهٔ رویت
روان ز چشمه چشم من است شط فراتی
خدای عالم و آدم مربّی همه اشیاء
ترا وفا بدهد یا مرا ز غصه نجاتی
حیات من نز جان و ممات من نز مرگ است
من او وصال حیات من به فراق مماتی
بوقت مرگ کشودی زپرسشم لب شیرین
چنانکه باز بمانم ز نو دمیده حیاتی

بجود وجهك ____ فرضاً على ____ في الصلواتِ

My Head in the Dust

I will lay my head in the dust before your face.
My idol, this is the holy law I embrace.

You are the Ka'aba that I long to circle 'round.
A river of tears falls from my eyes to the ground.

So don't ask me why I'm drunk: Just look at your eyes!
Don't tell me that I've lost my mind. Look at your face!

O Lord of the worlds! Bend his heart, so unbending!
Or else, release me from this grief where I am drowned.

No life flows from my soul, my tomb brings no ending.
To be with you is life, and separation death.

As I lay dying, your lips moved to speak a word
of care, and that is the one thing that gives me breath.

ای خفته رسید یار برخیز   از خود بنشان غبار برخیز
هین بر سر مهر و لطف آمد   ای عاشق زار یار برخیز
آمد بر تو طبیب غم‌خوار   ای خسته دل نزار برخیز
ای آنکه خمار یار داری   آمد مه غم‌گسار برخیز
ای آنکه به هجر مبتلائی   شد موسم وصل یار برخیز
ای آنکه خزان فسرده کردت   اینک آمد بهار برخیز
هان سال نو و حیات تازه است
ای مرده لاش پار برخیز

Sleeper!

Wake up, sleeper! Your lover's come for you!
Rouse yourself, brush those cobwebs from your hair

Gentle Love is here, and brings you kindness
Miserable lover, your Love stands near

Comfort awaits at the side of your bed
Sit up, throw off your grief—not one more tear!

Suffering, separate, lying there cold,
embrace your lover, who loves without fear

Wan and wasted, starved to death by the Fall,
Get up! Get up! At last the Spring is here

Our time's renewed, for life is always new
Rise! Rise up! You corpse of that old, dead year!

چشم مستش کرد عالم را خراب
هر که دید افتاد اندر پیچ و تاب

گردش چشم وی اندر هر نظر
می رباید حبهٔ اهل‌الباب

گو چه آید زین دل مجنون محض
کوزده در خیمهٔ لیلی قباب

خیمهٔ آتش‌نشینان پر شرر
آتش با شعله زد در هر حجاب

گر نه باشد نار موسی در ظهور
از چه گل محمود و اندر اضطراب

خواهم از ساقی بجامم طعمه‌ای
تا بگویم با تو سرّ ما اجاب

هان بنگر بر ما بعین باصره
تا ببینی وجه حق را بی نقاب

آمد از شطر عمائی در نزول
با تجلّی رُخی چون آفتاب

چشم مستش کرد عالم را خراب

His Drunken Eyes

His drunken eyes have wasted all the land!
Whoever gazes at him cannot stand!

He turns his head, and one glance from his eyes
will turn to sand the wisdom of the wise

Madder than Majnun, Layli's tent he flees
to throw his heart at any opened hand

The goldsmith's tent glows bright from his fire-brand
All veils now burn away at his demand

He holds the flame Moses could not withstand
It's not that bush—so why fear his command?

So come, and fill my cup! That's my demand!
I'll spill his secrets—I know them first-hand

Open your eyes! Gaze at us if you can,
and see the face of God! Do you understand?

Naked glory fills our universe and
like the sun sheds light on every land.

ایا عاشقان ایا عاشقان، شد آشکارا حجت حق

رفع حجب گردید هان، از قدرت رب الفلق

خیزید کایندم بابها، ظاهر شده و جز خدا

بنگر بصد لطف و صفا، آن روی روشن چون شفق

یعنی ز خلاق زمان، شد اینجهان جسم و جان

روز قیام است ای مهان، معدوم شد دلیل غسق

آمد زمان راستی، کژی شد اندر کاستی

آن شد که آن میخواستی، از عدل و ما انون و نسق

شد از میان جور و ستم، هنگام لطف است و کرم

ایدون بجای سهم و ستم، شد جانشین قوت و رمق

علم حقیقی شد عیان، شد جهل معدوم از میان

برگو بشیخ اندر زمان، برخیز و بهم زن ورق

بو دار پی عمری اژگون، وضع جهان از چند چون

هان شیر آمد جای خون، باید بگو دایی نه طبق

گرچه بماند از ملل، ظاهر شده شاه دول

لکن بلطف لم یزل، برها ند از ایشان غلق

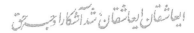

Lovers!

Lovers! Creation veils his face no more!
Lovers, look! He himself is visible!

See! The face of God glows with glory:
Look, lovers! Bright, pure, blinding, beautiful!

Who made the cosmos turns earth green once more.
Rise! Rise from that dark so miserable!

The day of truth is here! Lies have turned to dust!
Order, justice, law are now possible.

Smashed, the despot's fist! God's hand opens:
grace pours down—not sorrow, pain, and trouble

Minds in darkness now burn light with knowledge
Tell the priest: Shut your book! Lock the temple!

Hatred and doubt once poisoned all the world.
The bloodied cup holds milk now—pure, ample!

Let nations hear who's come to set them free:
Broken the chain, and smashed the manacle!

پادشه عشق ندا میکند   در رهِ معشوق صدا میکند

در صفتِ طلعت انوار او   خامه توصیف حیا میکند

هر که ز اسرار وے آگه شود   لاجرمش جان بفدا میکند

شمس که در روز ضیاءِ رخش   دہر پر از نور جلا میکند

سوی غمش رقص کنان میرود   هر که تمنّاے لقا میکند

دیدن رویش فقر را تمام   غرقه دریائے فنا میکند

این نه منم مادح رویش ورا   جمله ذرّات ثنا میکند

هر که ز الّای وے آگه شود

خویش در این مرحله لا میکند

The King of Love

I hear the King of Love calling
me to the path of endless love.

My pen, it dares not try explain
the dazzle of his face above.

Everyone who learns that secret
wants to throw his life away.

More than the sun, His face beams bright,
lights the earth, even at noonday.

His longing lovers start their dance,
with joy embrace calamity.

His face, that sacred looking glass,
reflects for us God's clarity.

The poor when once they see his face
are drowned in wealth and luxury.

Look! I am not the only one—
each atom sings his majesty.

Find this God, and you will become
the "No" before every other god.

صمدم ز عالم سرمدم، احدم ز منبع لاحدم
پے اہل افتد آمدم هلمّوا اِلَیَّ المقبلا

قبسات نارِ شئتی اناذا الستُ بربکم،
بگذر ز ز ساحتِ قدسیان کہ شنو صفیر بلی بلی

منم آن ظهورِ سیمینے، هم آن منیتے لے منی؛
منم آن سفینہ‌ی اَمِنی، و لقد ظهرتُ مجلجلا

شجر مرقع جان منم، ثمر عیان و نهان منم
ملک الملوکِ جهان منم، و لی البیان و قد علا

شهدائی طلعتِ نارِ من بدوید سوی دیارِ من،
ستر جان کنید نثارِ من کہ منم شہنشہ کربلا

طلعات قدس بشارتی که جمال حق شده بر ملا

بزن ای صبا تو بساحتش بجره غمزدگان صلا

هله ای طوائف منتظر از غایت شه مقتدر

مه مستتر شده مشتهر متنبها متجللا

شده طلعت صمدی عیان که بپاکنف علم بیان

زگمان و هم جهانیان جبروت اقدسه عتلا

بسر یر عزت فرخ نشان بنشسته آن شه بی نشان

بزد ای صلا به بلاکشان که گروه مدعی الولا

چو کسی طریق مرا رود کنمش ندا که خبر شود

که هر آنکه عاشق من بود نبرد ز محنت و ابتلا

کسی از نجد اطاعتم نه گرفت جبل ولایتم

کنمش بعید ز ساحتم دهمش بقهر ببادلا

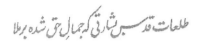

Listen!

Listen, holy people! I have good news for you!
His light has dawned. His beauty calls us to his side.

Listen, you who are waiting! The moon was hidden;
it shines now glorious. His grace is open wide.

I see His deathless face, I hear His words proclaimed,
and there I find a heaven pure and sanctified.

The unseen King above sits on the throne of Glory,
calls out to suffering folk: "You who are my pride!

But if you walk this path of love, I warn you now:
In anguish and calamity you will reside.

If you cannot bear this, you've not held fast my cord,
and with the winds of doubt I will cast you aside.

I am timeless. I am placeless, too. Rush here then—
to my place. Be on time—for these are sacred things.

When, from the flames, I call out: "Am I not your Lord?"
"Thou art, Thou art," the angels' answer rings.

I am manifest. I am hidden. Every gift is mine.
I am Life! I am Salvation! I am—the King of kings.

I am the Lord of Hosts! The Ark that Noah built!
I am that Self without a self. I rule all things.

I am the Prince of Karbalá—my face ablaze:
Give me your hearts—Then give your heads! Become
    holy beings!

جذبات شوقك الجمت بسلاسل الغم والبلا
همه عاشقان شکسته دل که دهند جان بره ولا

اگر آن صنم زره ستم پے کشتنم نہد قدم
لقد استقام بسیفه فلقد رضیت بما رضیٰ

سحر آن نگار ستمگرم قدمی نهاد به بسترم
فاذا رایت جماله طلع الصباح کانما

نه چو زلفِ غالیه بار او، نه چو چشمِ فتنه شعار او
شده نافه بہمه ختن شد کافری بہ ہمہ ختا

تو که غافل ازمی و شاهدی بے مردِ عابدِ زاهدی
چه کنم که کافر و جاحدی ز خلوصِ نیتِ اصفیا

تو و ملک و جاهِ سکندری من و رسم و راہِ قلندری
اگر آن نکوست تو در خوری وگر این بداست مرا سزا

بمرادِ زلفِ معلقی پے اسپ و زینِ مہ سرقی
همه عمر منکرِ مطلقی ز فقیرِ فارغِ بے نوا

بگذر ز منزلِ ما و من بگزین بملکِ فنا وطن
فاذا فعلت کمثل ذا فلقد بلغت بما تشآء

Running After You

So many will die of grief in their chains,
trembling with desire, running after you.

Although my true love comes to ravish me,
I'll stand before his sword, and gladly too.

My cruel lover invades my bed at dawn,
and I see beauty—the sunrise breaks through.

No pagan in China has such roguish eyes.
No musk compares to his hair wet with dew.

You ride past God and common folk careless—
just women, horse and saddle in your view.

You scorn this wine, you curse who pours it, to
follow hollow penance. What can I do?

I'll walk the beggar's path—though bad—it's mine.
It's Alexander's road that you pursue.

Ride past my camp, on your road to nowhere.
May you have all you wish, for it's your due.

افتتح یا مفتح الابواب	در وصل تو می‌زنند اجاب
کم بقوا ناظرین خلف الباب	چه شود گر بر تو ره یابند
طال طول فهم وراء حجاب	تا کی از حضرت تو صبر و شکیب
از ه نظرة بلا جلباب	در پس پرده تا بسی حسرت
مالدیهم سوی القاک ثواب	از تو غیر از تو مدعایی نیست
ما لهم من لدی سواک مثاب	سکردانیم هوایی ثم صوی
خرقوا الحجب وارتقوا الاسباب	از سبب ها گذشته‌اند و حجب
بکشا از جمال خویش نقاب	بنما آفتاب را بی ابر
خشک مغزان شوند اولوا الالباب	تا بمانند عاقلان حیران
هوشیاران شوند مست و خراب	با خود آیند بیخودان هوا
بنده و خواجه در هم آویزند	
لا عبید یری و لا ارباب	

Friends Are Knocking At the Door

Gatekeeper! Friends are knocking at the door.
Open the door! Why not open the door?

What is so wrong with letting them come in?
Why must they wait in the dark corridor?

How long do you think they can be patient?
How long should they stay there and pace the floor?

At least, why don't you raise the window curtain?
Just peek out for once to show your face.

They want nothing from you, except yourself.
The only thing they beg for is your grace.

Outside, they got drunk on love—then sober.
They didn't care. They're longing for your place.

They dropped their veils, forgot their desires,
gave up their search, and stripped to nudity.

Burn off the clouds now and show us the sun.
Pull off the veil. Let us see your beauty:

So then, the wise will be struck dumb,
and the fools will find their wisdom:

The selfish know their true Self then,
the saints will all get drunk with them:

No servant and no Lord will be,
Master and slave as one will be.

قدمی نهی تو به بسترم سحری ز فیض خود از کرم
بهوای قرب تو بر پرم به دو بال همت بجناحتی
برهانیم چو از این مکان بکشانیم سوی لامکان
گذرم ز جان و جهانیان که تو جان و جان ده خلقتی

بدیار عشق تو مانده‌ام ز کسے ندیده عنایتی
بغریبیم نظری فکن که تو پادشاه ولایتی

گنهی بود مگر ای صنم که ز سر عشق تو دم زنم
فهجرتنی و قتلتنی و اخذتنی بجنایتی

شده راه طاقت و صبر طی بچشم فراق تو تا بکی
همه بند بند مراچو نی بود از غم تو حکایتی

عجز العقول لدرک هلاک النفوس لوهمه
بکمال تو که برد رهی نبود بجز تو نهایتی

چو صبا برت گذر آورد ز بلاکشان خبر آورد
رخ زرد و چشم تر آورد چه شود کنی تو عنایتی

بی یار عشق تو مانده ام ز کسی ندیده عنایتی !

I Am Lost

I am lost in the heartland of your love,
and yet you do not even seem to care

Look down in pity at this foreigner,
you truest ruler of the kingdoms here,

and tell me, love, how have I sinned, and where?
And why, my idol, does your love prepare

with each breath to banish me, strip me bare
like some murderer exiled to nowhere?

I have waited for you day after day.
I'm weary now. I'm wasted, worn away

to bone, a flute that sighs away my care—
sorrows sung to the wind, and lost in air.

Is there a mind that knows your perfection?
A passion to utter your perfection?

A path that leads me to your perfection?
Beyond you, nothing, and no direction

And when the wandering wind reaches you,
it carries our tormented words to you

Look at these tear-filled eyes, this pallid face—
Can you refuse them? Whom would it disgrace?

Will you not come at daybreak to my bed,
with kindness ravish me, and end my dread?

Lift me, love, on the wings of my desire
Lift me to you, to safety in your fire

Only take me up, away from this place
Set me down in the place that is no place

Yet keep me close to you, far from strife,
since in this empty world, I have no life

بخیالت ای نکو رو مبتلا م باشد این دل

بجمالت ای نکو خو، بکلام باشد این دل

چو نموده ای بافسون، بدل حزین پر خون

که مسلسل از نظاره به هیام باشد این دل

بجمال حسن رویت، بتار مشک مویت

بهار بزم کویت، بمرام باشد این دل

چو بخوانیش به محضر، بر پیش بعز منظر

بجلال و شوکت و فر بنظام باشد این دل

چو بجذب روی مهوش شده ام غریق آتش

نشود دگر که سرخوش بغمام باشد این دل

به تلطف و تکرم، به تعطف و ترحم

بر باز ما تو هم، که همام باشد این دل

چو ز ما سوی برانی، ز خودش بخود رسانی

ز بلاء خود چشایی نے، بدام باشد این دل

ز دلم شراره بارد که نسب زنار دارد

ز چه رو مگر نیارد که بکام باشد این دل

This Heart

This heart, this heart, it thinks of only you.
This heart, I swear, it sings for only you.

Wounded and bleeding, enchanted, undone:
this heart, I swear, it sings for only you.

The musk in your hair, the spell of your face:
this heart, I swear, delights in only you.

And just to be in heaven standing there,
this heart finds its rightful place in glory.

The moonlight of your eyes, and drenched in fire:
dark clouds now flee from this heart's ecstasy.

Be kind, generous! Take pity, take care!
End this heart's pathetic agitation.

Driven from everything, drawn just to you:
freed from death in tasting your affliction.

Let sparks fly! This heart's father is the fire.
This joyful heart will burn hot with desire.

غیر او مشهود نبود در عیان
محو موهومات شد اندر بیان
اسم اعلی از نَسَمی شد مُتین
شد برون فرقان حق از آستین
رَبِّ اعظم رَبِّ اَعلی شان او
رَبِّ اکبر روضهٔ رضوان او
عرش‌ها با رفعت شان بها
بس ستائرها مرفع از سما
الله الله ای قدیم لم یزل
قادرِ حَیِّ عطوفِ لامثل
یک نظر فرما به انظار رحیم
زنده کردان بندهٔ اَعظمِ الرَّمیم
تا نمایم نطق از اسرار تو
در نظر آورم اَضمار تو
جز توام مقصود نبود در بنا
جز توام معبود ناید در شنا
سر وحدت را تو فرما آشکار
چند کردم در سما خورشیدوار
ای حبیب حُبّ محبوب بها
جذب فرما این عبید مبتلا
بر بساط عزّ وحدت مستقر
ساز از الطاف خود بی حدّ و مر

غیر او مشهود نبود در عیان

No One Else

His words—his Bayán!—broke my fantasy
Now no one else, him only do I see

The name of God burns brightly in his name
as God once burned in that pillar of flame

Greatest of masters, most lordly of lords!
Whose garden of gardens lies beyond words

Exalted seats that rise beyond the sky:
Thrones called Bahá, rank upon rank so high

You are my God! You are, you always were
Eternal, Almighty, Grace without peer

With kindness look on one who is alone
Grant new life to this dead, this rotting bone

Let me freely tell your mysteries here
and make your deepest, inmost meanings clear

What other aim or end is there but you
Who else for me to laud, adore but you

You spoke the secret: Oneness is One
Why then must I go lost, alone, undone?

Bahá's loved one loves and is loved. Dear Lover,
take your slave, take me now, this sufferer

Kindness blossoms like a gentle flower
Harmony stands on the carpet of power

عشق به هر لحظه ندا می‌کند   بر همه موجود صدا می‌کند
هر که هوای ره ما می‌کند   کی حذر از موج بلا می‌کند؟
پای نهد بر لب دریای من
هندوی نوبت زن بام توام   طایر سرگشته به دام توام
مرغ شباویز به شام توام   محو زخود، زنده به نام توام
کشته زمین درد من و مای من

کعبهٔ من خاک سر کوی تو   مشعله افروز جهان، روی تو
سلسلهٔ جان، خم گیسوی تو   قبلهٔ دل، طاق دو ابروی تو
زلف تو در دیر، چلیپای من

شیفتهٔ حضرت اعلاستم   عاشق دیدار دلارا ستم
راهرو وادی سوداستم   از همه بگذشته تو را خواستم
پر شده از عشق تو اعضای من

تا کی و کی پند نیوشی کنم؟   چند نهان بلبل‌سلم پوشی کنم؟
چند ز هجر تو خموشی کنم؟   پیش کسان زهد فروشی کنم؟
تا که شود راغب کالای من

خرقه و سجاده به دور افکنم   باده به مینای بلور افکنم
شعشعه در وادی طور افکنم   بام و در از عشق به شور افکنم
بر در میخانه بود جای من

عشق علم کوفت به ویرانه‌ام   داد صلا بر در جانانه‌ام
بادهٔ حق ریخت به پیمانه‌ام   از خود و عالم همه بیگانه‌ام
حق طلبد همت والای من

ساقی میخانهٔ بزم «الست»   ریخت به هر جام چو صهبا ز دست
ذره صفت شد همه ذرات پست   باده زماست شد و کشتی ست
از اثر نشئهٔ صهبای من

آتش عشقت چو برافروخت دود سوخت مرا مایهٔ هر هست و بود
کفر و مسلمانیم از من زدود تا به خم ابرویت آدم نبود
فرق نه از کعبه کلیسای من

کلک ازل تا به ورق زد رقم گشت هم آغوش چو لوح و قلم
نامده خلقی به وجود از عدم بر تن آدم چو دمیدند دم
مهر تو بد در دل شیدای من

دست قضا چون گل آدم سرشت مهر تو در مزرعه سینه بکشت
عشق تو گردید مرا سرنوشت فارغم اکنون ز جحیم و بهشت
نیست به غیر از تو تمنای من

با قدمیم از یاد خود و فانیم جرعه‌کش بادهٔ ربانیم
سوختهٔ وادی حیرانیم سالک صحرای پریشانیم
تا چه رسد بر دل رسوای من

بر در دل تا ارنی کوش شدم جلوه‌کنان بر سر آن کو شدم
هر طرفی گرم تمنا هو شدم او همگی من شد و من او شدم
من دل و او گشت دلارای من

ای به سر زلف تو سودای من و ز غم هجران تو غوغای من
لعل لبت شهد مصفای من عشق تو بگرفت سراپای من
من شده ام تو آمده بر جای من

گر چه بسی رنج غمت برده ام جام پیاپی ز بلا خورده ام
سوخته جانم اگر افسرده ام زنده دلم گر چه ز غم مرده ام
چون لب تو هست مسیحای من

گنج منم بانی مخزن توئی سیم منم صاحب معدن توئی
دانه منم صاحب خرمن توئی هیکل من چیست اگر من توئی؟
گر تو منی چیست هیولای من؟

من شدم از مهر تو چون ذره پست و ز قدح باده عشق تو مست
تا به سر زلف تو داریم دست تا تو منی من شده ام خودپرست
سجده که من شده اعضای من

دل اگر از تست چرا خون کنی؟ ور ز تو نبود ز چه مجنون کنی؟
دم به دم این سوز دل افزون کنی تا خودیم را همه بیرون کنی
جای کنی در دل شیدای من

ای به سر زلف تو سودای من

From Those Locks

Now from those locks must all my madness hang
Your ruby lips have taught me love's sweet pang
From head to toe your love about me sang
Cut off from you, how loud my weeping rang
    I'm lost: You have destroyed my place

Although you brought me sad adversity
and I drank my cup of calamity,
my soul burns in its frozen cavity,
my heart lives on, that died in misery
    Your lips are my Messiah's grace

You guard the vault where I am its treasure
You keep the mine where I am its silver
I am the seed, and you are the sower
But whose body is this, if you're its owner?
    What's this soul? You have filled its place

Your love has made of me a speck of dust
One single cup of wine—I'm drunk with lust
Since I have seized and hold your locks in trust:
Myself I praise—You I praise—I praise us!
    I lie lost in my arms' embrace

If my heart is yours, why would you tear it?
And if not yours, why should you impair it?
With each breath you feed the flame in it,
consuming what remains of me in it
    Make it your joyful dwelling-place!

When your love's fire grew incandescent,
Being and Having burnt from my essence
Heathen and Muslim from my heart were sent
Prostrate, I lie beneath your eyebrow's tent
    The very Ka'aba is my place

When the divine feather wrote upon the page
and pen kissed paper in love's knowledge,
when Nothingness heard not Being's homage
and His breath blew over Adam's image,
    my heart felt even then love's trace

When the divine hand molded Adam's clay,
your love sowed its seed in my breast that day,
your love became my foreknown, fated way
Not hell, not heaven can lead me astray
    You alone are whom I embrace

I am eternal, yet destroyed in mind
From this good cup I sip a lordly wine
In the valley of doubt I'm burnt to brine
A wanderer, to exile's wastes confined
    What may befall me in disgrace?

Since that day my heart cried out, *Behold me!*
and I stepped in that street for all to see,
gadding about, a shameless debauchee,
He was all myself, all myself was he—
    His jewel set in my heart's palace

In the dust of my Ka'aba you now dwell
Your face lights the dark world with its dazzle
The waves of your hair my soul's manacle
The arch of your eyebrows my heart's idol
    Your locks my cross in sacred space

I'm the captive of his high holiness
I love his lovely heart's expressiveness
I walk through the valley of my madness
wanting no other but you to caress
    Love fills me with your sweet embrace

Then how much longer must I be restrained,
my feigned indifference to you still maintained?
How long must agitation be contained?
A prudish piety, how long ordained?
    My wares banned from the marketplace?

I'll drop my robe, my prayer mat I'll discard,
drink till I'm drunk, and none of them regard
My passion will fill their house, roof to yard
Mt. Sinai's flame grows bright, for I'm its bard
    By the tavern gate, there's my place!

Love's flag flies above my devastation
At Love's gate stands his annunciation
Truth brims my cup with intoxication
Estranged from myself, from every nation
    God bids me run this noble race

The tavern's servant served us at the feast
Red wine was poured and poured and never ceased,
until the wine grew drunk and went to yeast
And all were turned to dust, even the least,
    fermented by my wine's embrace

Night and day have we heard Love's voice proclaim:
It's Love that calls each being by its name
Whoever wants to make our way his aim
shall find that suffering's waves are not tame,
    nor will the shore give his foot place

I am the slave on your roof keeping time,
I am the frightened bird snared by your lime,
the nightingale silent in your night-time,
the axis that stands for your name, Sublime
    Not I, not we—That agony's erased!

Notes

Notes

by Amin Banani

IT IS NOT ACCIDENTAL that we have decided to begin this collection of Táhirih's work with this poem (p. 47). Jascha Kessler, who shaped this piece into an English poem, has given it the title "Look Up!" which is certainly appropriate. But, it should be remembered that classical poems were never given titles in Persian literature, but simply stood on their own. So, this title, as all other titles given to the poems in this book, is not Táhirih's. It has been added here simply to allow easy reference.

This remarkable poem is written as a *ghazal*, but it departs so fully from traditional concepts as to be startling in its newness—even today. A ghazal is a monorhymed, lyric poem devoted to the subject of love: either earthly love or mystical divine love. Persian mystical love poems developed an elaborate traditional vocabulary of tropes such as nightingales, wine, moon, descriptions of

Look Up!
English Poem by Jascha Kessler

هان صبح بُدی دَم ســرمزد آغازِ تنفّس !

Amin Banani

the beloved's face, etc. Some of Persia's finest poetry has been produced in the traditional ghazal form. The ghazal became the dominant form of Persian poem in the 1300s, with Hafez, and remained so for centuries.

In "Look Up!" Táhirih discards the traditional tropes altogether to produce a poem that is as far as can be imagined from lyric, love verse. She chooses new words, new images, and new concepts. The rhythm and sound of the poem are also startling. In the original language, her lines end with stressed, sibilant rhymes that are deliberately jarring, dissonant, and powerful.

This is a poem that is unusual even among Táhirih's own work. While "Look Up!" expresses a deep longing for a new world, Táhirih has ignored lyric themes of love. The non-lyric use of the ghazal form is not unknown in Persian literature. Perhaps one-third of the ghazals of Rumi are non-lyric. What is startling here is the ferociously anti-clerical sentiment she expresses and the broad universality of her vision of a new age.

Táhirih was born into a clerical family of considerable importance in Qazvin. Her father and uncle were influential *mujtahids* (high ranking religious officials) who had amassed considerable fortunes and held religious sway over certain quarters of the city. Táhirih was raised in a strictly religious environment and completed higher religious studies in the best theological schools. Therefore, this poem is all the more remarkable for its frank rejection of the ulama and of religious vocations. Her merciless condemnation of mosque, priest, and pulpit could not be more complete. Her anti-clerical statements are unexpectedly modern, and they might have even been written today.

Since the whole orthodox Shi'i ulama stood against

Notes

both the Shaykhi school and the Bábí religion, these sentiments might be understandable. But the extent of Táhirih's emotion may also suggest a personal dimension, beyond abstract ideas. We should remember that both her husband (from whom she separated) and her uncle (whose murder she was falsely accused of arranging) were outspoken enemies of the Báb.

Bábí themes of the end of the age of ignorance and war are clearly evident from the first line of the poem. But in the last three couplets, Táhirih introduces ideas of equality, justice, search after truth, universal friendship, and the reconciliation of ancient hatreds. This is truly astonishing, since such ideas were not prominent among the Bábís of Táhirih's time and would only be explicitly developed in later Bahá'í teachings. This poem is a stunning testimony to the great spirit of this visionary woman.

Just Let the Wind ...
English Poem by Anthony A. Lee

اگر بباد دهسم زلفت عنبر آسارا

IN THIS SHORT POEM, (p. 49) Táhirih makes use of the traditional images that are found in classical Persian poems—perfumed hair, gazelles in the wilderness, painted eyes, dawn, and mirror. But, she has molded these tropes to serve an unexpected purpose. This is an exceptionally forceful poem in which Táhirih celebrates her own charismatic power.

A few women poets in Persian history—among them Rabi'ih and Mahsti of Ganja—have pursued this theme in their work, insisting on the power of their gender to attract and subdue. Being female, far from becoming a

Amin Banani

disability, becomes the source of power and dominance. Such poems were celebrated by scholars, but also disapproved of for brazenly breaking the limits of propriety. This has not deterred Táhirih from writing along these same lines, however.

The last lines of the poem bring to mind the famous story told by Attar, in his celebrated poem *The Conference of the Birds*. The Shaykh of San'an (or Sam'an), a pious Muslim, falls hopelessly in love with a Christian girl. She demands that he forsake his religion as proof of his love—drink wine, burn the Qur'an, herd pigs, etc. He complies with all of her demands for the sake of love. Still, in the end, he is forgiven and saved because he walked the path of love so faithfully.

Here Táhirih reverses Attar's story, announcing that the Christian girls (or nuns, perhaps) will rush to follow her religion if she should simply chance to pass by a church.

He Has Come!
English Poem by Jascha Kessler

آمد او با جلوه‌های سرمدی

HERE TÁHIRIH SPEAKS directly to the fulfillment of Islamic prophecies by the Báb. The first lines of the poem (p. 51) literally read:

> He has come with eternal brilliance.
> and made the face of Ahmad (i.e., Muhammad) to appear again.

This poem does not take the form of a ghazal, but is written in rhyming couplets (*aa, bb, cc,* etc.), a form called *masnavi* in Persian. The sixth couplet is Arabic.

Notes

In this couplet, Táhirih plays on the words *jamil* (beautiful) and *jalil* (majestic, glorious) as two of the attributes of God. In the final two couplets, the open mention of Bayán (the Báb's major book) and *Esm-e A'lá* (the Name of the Exalted One) leaves no doubt that "He" who has come is the Báb.

Proclamation
English Poem by Jascha Kessler

THIS SHORT POEM (p. 53), a fragment (*qat'a*), is also written in rhyming couplets, as the previous one. Yet in a few lines, it achieves tremendous power. Táhirih assumes the voice and persona of God to make her proclamation.

Here we have another fearless rejection of conventional and traditional religion. In the last line of the poem, the poet speaks with a "Divine plural" pronoun. Literally: "Our Cause has been made manifest from the letters *kaf* ["B"] and *nun* ["E"]. She ends with a quotation from the Qur'an: "Say: Those who are from God to Him shall return." (Qur'an 2:151)

The King Walked In
English Poem by Anthony A. Lee

HERE TÁHIRIH has produced a formal poem (p. 55), using traditional and classical formulae, that is intended as a song of praise or tribute. The object of her praise is ostensibly the Báb.

Amin Banani

The poem makes use of the most formal, panegyric language to offer its praise. The effect of the verse reminds one of a fanfare of trumpets that might announce the arrival of a royal personage. Indeed, the subject of the poem is the arrival of the Prophet, even though he is unrecognized and unseen—except by his true lovers, by the mountains, and by the prophets of the past who rush forth out of history to attain his presence.

It is notable, however, that Táhirih uses the Arabic word *Bahá* (here translated as *Glory)* twice in this short poem. We might suspect this to be a reference to Bahá'u'lláh, who was a prominent Bábí leader, and later the founder of the Bahá'í Faith to which most Bábís were eventually converted. Naturally, it is impossible to say that with any certainty in this case. However, Táhirih was closely acquainted with Bahá'u'lláh. He had, in fact, arranged for her to be rescued from imprisonment in her father's house in Qazvin in late 1847, after she had been falsely accused of complicity in the murder of her uncle Mullá Muhammad-Taqí Baraghání. Bahá'u'lláh had her brought to Tehran, and he had protected her in his house for some time.

Táhirih's relationship with many of the early leaders of the Bábí movement was problematic. She clashed on occasion with a number of prominent Bábí men, including with Quddús. There is no question, however, about the admiration and unambiguous respect that Táhirih showed to Bahá'u'lláh who was her protector and her host.

Notes

Start Shouting!
English Poem by Anthony A. Lee

هلا مژده کرده عمانیان یکسو شهید طوبامرولا

THIS IS ANOTHER celebratory poem (p. 58). But this verse, rather than remaining formal, embodies all of the joyous, ecstatic emotion associated with the discovery of new Faith. Táhirih's exultation knows no bounds. She has no question about the victory of the Cause she champions. Her voice is absolutely triumphant.

The first line of the poem reads literally:

> Glad tidings, people of *'Amá!*

The use of the Arabic word *'amá* (literally, "cloud"; meaning here, "ethereal cloud," "celestial cloud," or perhaps "the cloud of Divine Revelation") is extremely rare in the history of Persian poetry. It is also the subject of one of the early poems of Bahá'u'lláh *Rashh-i 'Ama* (literally, "the sprinkling of the cloud"), which poured forth in the Síyáh-Chál dungeon in Tehran where he was imprisoned in 1852.

In the fourth couplet of the poem, Táhirih makes a double reference to Fars and to Tehran, as both having been set afire by the spirit. Fars is the southern province of Persia which includes Shiraz; the city of the Báb. Tehran is the capital, and the city of Bahá'u'lláh.

One of the most universal metaphors of Persian mystical and lyrical poetry is that of the sleepless nightingale that sings all night for love of the rose. The nightingale is the symbol of the lover who longs for the Beloved—who is God, or some reflection of His beauty. In a revolutionary gesture, Táhirih explicitly rejects this metaphor in the next couplet. Since she says it is dawn, not nighttime, she prefers the symbol of the cockerel (rooster) who crows out his love for the sun. Again, we have the use of the word *bahá* (glory).

The following verse makes reference to a famous passage of the Qur'an (7:172), and the tradition of the Day of *Alast*. On that day, God gathered together in pre-existence all the souls of every human being who would ever be born. He asked them: "Am I not your Lord?" and they all replied: "Thou art." So, every soul has at one time seen his Lord, and will recognize him again.

The tenth couplet of the English translation is missing from the Persian calligraphy:

دو هزار احمد مصطفی ز بروق آن شه با صفا
شده مضطرب شده در خفا متدشرا متزملا

The poem is a celebration of the mission of the Báb, and perhaps of Bahá'u'lláh as well. Táhirih expresses ecstatic joy at the unlimited possibilities embodied in a new age.

Morning Breezes
English Poem by Anthony A. Lee

This poem (p. 61) is unusual in Táhirih's work because of its references to specific people and places. Persian classical poems seldom make specific references, preferring instead to use familiar images and metaphors to express their themes.

Again we find a reference to the name of Bahá'u'lláh (*bahá*) and to the ethereal cloud of Divine Revelation.

Notes

Táhirih mentions also the city of Tehran. She then makes the unexpected specific reference to the Bábís of Núr (light)—Núr being the name for the part of Mazandárán where Bahá'u'lláh was from. All of these references serve to reinforce the impression that the entire poem is addressed to Bahá'u'lláh, rather than to the Báb.

It should be emphasized, however, that this is only an impression. The poem stands well on its own as a powerful statement, regardless of the specific question of to whom it may have been addressed.

Point by Point
English Poem by Anthony A. Lee

THIS POEM (p. 64) is discussed at some length in the introduction to this volume (see, pp. 21-26). Of all the poems of Táhirih that have become familiar to Iranian and South Asian audiences, this one is the most famous. It has been set to music many times and performed. The poem takes the form of a traditional ghazal: its subject is love. Presumably, the poem is addressed to the Báb.

This might be regarded as Táhirih's signature poem in those countries where her work is known. It is, of course, also one of Táhirih's masterpieces.

Táhirih begins with a double rhyme in the first half-line, and a meter for the poem that is so lyrical that it almost demands to be sung, rather than recited.

The power of the poem rests on the doubling of words:

> . . . word by word,
> point by point

so that the poet produces double and quadruple rhymes. The Persian rhyming was, of course, impossible to reproduce in English translation. Moreover, each stanza of the poem ends with a familiar rhyming, Persian idiom.

However, Táhirih has used this complicated scheme to produce a work that reads as an effortless, facile love poem—utterly simple and enchanting. It is a work that well deserves its appeal and popularity.

Your Brilliant Face
English Poem by Anthony A. Lee

لعماتُ وجهِكَ اَثَّرَ قَتْ شعاعُ طلعتِكَ اِغْرَا

IN THIS POEM (p. 67), Táhirih again makes use of the metaphoric Day of *Alast*, the primordial morning when a covenant was sealed between God and every individual human being. This morning she associates with her Beloved, whom she urges to raise the call of "Am I not your Lord?" so that she can respond. So, once more we see evidence of her impatience with things as they are and her desire for revolutionary change.

The first line of the poem as well as the second hemistich of the fourth and fifth lines are in Arabic, while the rest is in Persian. The poet quickly moves the verse into the full imagery of battle. Literally:

> I beat the war drums of calamity
> and armies of suffering camped at the gate of my heart

Also, she refers to the battle of Karbalá (682 A.D.) and the martyrdom of Imám Husayn, metaphorically referring to her own death cries during that battle.

Notes

The poem ends with a signature line, commonly used in ghazals. In this line, the poet makes use of her own pen name (Táhirih) as a poetic device. The final lines read, literally:

> You who are only a scale on the fish of perplexity, how can you make any claim on the Ocean of Being?
> Sit down with Táhirih so that you may hear wave after wave of the roaring of the Leviathan of "No."

The final word ("No," Arabic: *lá*) is a reference to the Muslim confession of faith (*shaháda*): There is *no* God but God . . . (*lá iláha illá* . . .)."

Browne published his full, Victorian, English-verse translation of this poem in 1891, and again in 1918. We include it here with his footnotes:[1]

> *The effulgence of thy face flashed forth and the rays of thy visage arose on high;*
> *Then speak the word, "Am I not your Lord?" and "Thou art, Thou art!" we will all reply.*[2]
> *The trumpet-call "Am I not?" to greet how loud the drums of affliction*[3] *beat!*
> *At the gates of my heart there tramp the feet and camp the hosts of calamity.*
> *That fair moon's love is enough, I trow, for me, for he laughed at the hail*[4] *of woe,*

---

1. Edward G. Browne, *Materials for the Study of the Bábí Religion* (Cambridge University Press, 1918) pp. 350-51.
2. See Qur'an vii, 171. The meaning is, "If you claim to be God, we will all accept your claim."—E.G.B.
3. There is a play on the word *balá*, which means "yea" and also "affliction."—E.G.B.
4. *Salá*, which I have translated "hail," means a general invitation or summons.—E.G.B.

Amin Banani

And triumphant cried, as he sunk below, "The Martyr of
  Karbalá am I.⁵
When he heard my death-dirge drear, for me he prepared,
  and arranged my gear for me;
He advanced to mourn at my bier for me, and o'er me
  wept right bitterly.
What harm if thou wilt the fire of amaze should'st set my
  Sinai-heart ablaze,
Which thou first mad'st fast in a hundred ways but to
  shake and shatter so ruthlessly?
To convene the guests to his feast of love all night from the
  angel host above
Peals forth this summons ineffable, "Hail, sorrow-stricken
  fraternity!"
Can a scale of the fish of amaze like thee aspire to enquire
  of Being's Sea?
Sit mute like Táhira, hearkening to the whale of "No" and
  its ceaseless sigh.⁶

A Beauty Mark
English Poem by Jascha Kessler

خال بکنج لب یکی طـــرّه مشک فام دو

THIS POEM (p. 69) takes the form of a riddle. This was not an unknown poetic form in the Persian classical tradition, but it was not commonly used. In this form, the poet introduces a riddle that the reader is supposed to solve, unraveling the various enigmatic clues that the poet playfully offers.

In this poem, Táhirih plays with the numbers one and two, the concepts of unity and duality, perhaps with

---

5. I.e., the Imám Husayn, of whom several of the Bábí leaders claimed to be a "Return."—E.G.B.
6. I.e., "Thou art a mere tiny scale on the smallest fish of the Ocean of Being, and even the Leviathans of that Ocean can but proclaim their own insignificance and non-existence."—E.G.B.

Notes

notions of "I" and "Thou." She evokes with it a series of paradoxical and contradictory images. But the images only puzzle and astonish the reader. The riddle is not easy to solve, and she provides no clue of an answer at the end.

One cannot resist the conclusion that Táhirih here is being deliberately mercurial and elusive. The poem is impish, and almost mischievously contrary. The reader is left in perplexity, but perhaps on the edge of a discovery.

Noqaba'í suggests that this poem was written in 1852, while Táhirih was under house arrest in the home of the *kalántar* of Tehran. She was interviewed there by two inquisitors—a mullá and *mohtaseb* (representative of the moral police)—both of whom recommended that she be sentenced to death. He writes that the second couplet is a reference to that interview.

The poem's fourth couplet, missing in the calligraphy, reads:

حامله خم ز دخت رز باده کشان به گرد او
طفل حرامزاده بین باب یکی و مام دو

The next lines in the Persian text read:

ساقی ماهروی من از چهٔ نشسته غافلی
باده بیار می بده نقد یکی و وام دو

My moon-faced cupbearer why are you sitting, inattentive?
Bring the wine, pass it around, cash is one and credit two.

This may also be a reference to Táhirih's meeting with her two inquisitors. She calls for three cups of (divine) wine: she will pay for her own (with love), but the other two (the priest and the judge) will need credit.

In Pursuit
English Poem by Anthony A. Lee

A HIGHLY LYRICAL POEM (p. 71), easily set to music, this is one of Táhirih's ghazals that portrays a pronounced feminine sensibility and tonality. The dual juxtapositions that create the tension and the structure of the poem are not resolved in the conventional and expected mystic fashion. Instead, Táhirih remains in her yearning, subservient place at the feet of her beloved to the end.

My Head in the Dust
English Poem by Anthony A. Lee

بجود و جهك ـــــــ فرضاً علی ـــــــ فی الصلواتی

THIS POEM (p. 73) provides an excellent example of Tahirih's use of two classical conventions of Persian poetry—*esteqbál* (poetic imitation) and *tazmin* (borrowing). Here she calls upon a familiar classical poem.

"My Head in the Dust" is similar in form and rhyme to a famous poem of Sa'di, the first line of which reads:

تو قدر آب چه دانی که در کنار فراتی

to qadr-e áb che dáni ke dar kenár-e Foráti

> How can you know the value of water,
>   you who are on the banks of the Euphrates?

We witness her creativity here, not in the form the poem takes, but in its contents. The familiar images take a radical, new turn.

Notes

In addition to imitating the formal aspects of Sa'di's poem, Tahirih also borrows his style of *molamma'* (bilingual poetry). The first and the tenth lines of the piece are Arabic, while the rest of the lines are in Persian.

The first lines use familiar images and might be translated literally to read:

> Prostration before your face is required of me when I
>   say my obligatory prayer.
> I would worship you even if you were *Lát* and *Manát*.

(*Lát* and *Manát* were two legendary idols worshiped in pre-Islamic Arabia that were destroyed by Muhammad.) The effect of the juxtaposition of these images of piety and idolatry is quite shocking.

In the next lines, Táhirih uses great skill to layer more familiar images with multiple meanings. Here the classical trope she calls on is the seductive eyes of the Beloved. Yet, Tahirih uses double meanings to create a chess metaphor, as well. Literally:

> Look in the mirror and see your own face (*rokh*=rooks).
> Then, don't ask me why I am astonished (checkmated).

The poem ends in joyous anticipation of death, and new life. Literally, again:

> At the moment of death you moved to answer
>   all my questions.
> And if I live, now I will have new life.

So, at the point of death, she is saved both by the movement of the Beloved's lips and the healing words that he speaks to her. Her death is transformed into life.

Amin Banani

Sleeper!
English Poem by Jascha Kessler

THIS IS A ROUSING, lyrical ghazal (p. 75) that almost demands to be sung, rather than simply recited. The poem is written in a simple, facile meter and with mono-rhymed line endings. It is a simple and unambiguous call for the reform, resurrection, and renewal of the corrupt and moribund social order of Táhirih's time.

Again, it is the content of the poem—as with so many of Táhirih's works—that is revolutionary. One of the most characteristic aspects of classical Persian poetry is a pervasive mode of melancholy. Classical verse is filled with themes of separation, hopelessness, and longing; the beloved is worshipped from afar, and the lover is seldom—if ever—actually united with the object of desire.

In stark contrast to the traditional mood, all of the images that Táhirih uses in this poem are joyous and happy. The poet chides the "sleeper" for her lethargy and urges her to cast off all sadness and depression. The happy moment of the arrival of the beloved one is imminent. Every image of suffering and separation is negated by the joyous proclamation.

At the end of the poem, Táhirih mentions Spring, the New Year of the Persian calendar. The old year is cast off, the New Year comes back to life. In fact, this poem may well have been written on the occasion of Naw-Rúz, the Persian (and later, the Bahá'í) New Year's Day. Or, perhaps, the poet is simply making reference to the spiritual renewal of the world, a symbolic New Year, which is the birth of a new social order. In any case, the last words of the poem reveal that the "sleeper" is actually a corpse that is resurrected with the coming of a New Day.

Notes

The fourth line is missing in the translation:

ای آ نکه خمار یار داری
آمد مه غمگسار برخیز

You who are drunk with the beloved
The grief-dispelling moon has come, arise!

His Drunken Eyes
English Poem by Jascha Kessler

چشم مستش کرد عالم را خراب

THE FIRST QUESTION that may occur to the reader upon reading this poem (p. 77) is: Whose drunken eyes? Who is being described here? For that matter: Who is speaking? And: Who is being addressed?

But, of course, these questions can have no final answers. Táhirih is making use of familiar tropes of Persian poetry to ask a different kind of question and to serve an entirely different purpose. In the classical tradition, amorous and even erotic references in poetry do not necessarily have any specific person or object in mind. And the desired ambiguity is further intensified by the absence of gender in Persian pronouns, so that the one addressed may be either male or female. In this case, we can say that, generally, Táhirih is discussing the spirit. But it would be futile to ask for a specific reference beyond that. It is Táhirih's purpose in this poem to portray a spiritual state or condition, not to describe an individual's face.

The poem begins by calling on the conventional image of the beloved's irresistible eyes. Next, she

Amin Banani

wonders at the power of the beloved's glance. Clearly, this is just one of his/her many powers.

This power of attraction, or love, gives rise to the trope of Layli and Majnun, the iconic lovers of the classical Persian tradition. Majnun's love is traditionally described in Persian and Arabic literature as a kind of divine madness.

The story of Layli gives rise to the imagery of her tent, which is the object of Majnun's desire. But this Majnun is so mad with love that he abandons the tent of his beloved to give himself to any passerby.

Then, we find that the tent is on fire, set aflame by the sparks of the goldsmith's hammer. Táhirih says that this fire must burn away all veils. The theme of the removal of veils is a *leitmotif* that runs through much of Táhirih's poetry. We remember here that the poet herself quite literally cast off her veil on a number of occasions, most famously at the Bábí conference at Badasht in 1848. In this poem we catch a glimpse of the meaning of that symbolic act.

The fire that burns away the veils next reminds the poet of the Burning Bush that Moses saw, and from which God spoke to him. The penultimate stanza of the poem calls again on the "removed-veil" trope. It reads literally:

> Look deeply with discerning eyes,
> so you may see the face of God without a veil.

The final stanza of the poem makes use of the unusual image of the billowing cloud, which is rarely found in classical Persian poetry. Again, it is reminiscent of Bahá'u'lláh's use of the same image in his Rashh-i 'Amá. The lines can be literally translated as:

> From the folds of this billowing cloud (*shatr-i 'amá*)
> has descended a face like the sun.

Notes

Lovers!
English Poem by Jascha Kessler

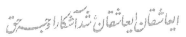

IN THIS GHAZAL (p. 79), Táhirih again makes use of the poetic convention of *tazmin* (borrowing) to begin her poem with the same words that are found in the first line of one of Rumi's well-known poems. But, while the opening words and the form of the poem echo the style of Rumi, the rhyme is distinctly different.

Here we have a triumphal declaration of the appearance of the Promised One, the Manifestation of God. The poet makes use of hard, consonant rhymes at the end of each line. The harsh rhymes in Persian emphasize the definitive finality of each statement. The effect is to provide a formal declaration of the Great Announcement.

In the first lines of the poem, Táhirih again calls on the motif of unveiling that is found so often in her poems. Here she declares that the face of God has been unveiled. The reader, of course, cannot help but recall the poet's own famous unveiling.

The second stanza invokes the word "glory" (Arabic: *bahá*), translated in the English poem as:

> The face of God glows with glory.

In the sixth stanza, Táhirih makes a bold anticlerical statement. In fact, she exults in rejecting the authority of the Shí'í ulama, who are supposed to be the learned of religion but are actually the purveyors of ignorance. Her rejection of the clerical tradition was fully informed, as well, by her own education within that tradition, and her own family position—her husband, her father, and her uncle (who was also her father-in-law) held high office among the ulama of Qazvin. The significance of such

Amin Banani

anticlerical statements would not have been lost on the clergymen of her time—which may explain part of their ferocious opposition to her message.

Yet, Táhirih ends the poem on a gentle note. The last lines read literally:

> Although he has come to warn the nations,
> yet he comes with kindness to end all anxiety.

The King of Love
English Poem by Anthony A. Lee

پادشه عشق ندا میکند

THIS POEM (p. 81) is a ghazal, a love poem. The strong amatory themes and the rhyming lyricism of the poem lend themselves to song. The rhyme of the poem is simple and strong—and this is reflected in the English translation.

In the first lines of the poem, Táhirih rhymes the words *nedá* and *sedá*, both of which mean "call" or "summons." The first word *nedá* refers to a summons from an unknown source; while *sedá* is the normal word for a cry or shout. So the attention of the reader is directed to a voice. The lines read literally:

> The king of love is sending out a *nedá*.
> In the path of the beloved it is heard as a *sedá*.

Beginning with the call of God, the poet leads us through the spiritual journey of the soul. In this short poem, a remarkable distance is covered: The second stanza expresses awe and bewilderment. The following stanzas then successively evoke sacrifice, enlightenment, calamity, knowledge, annihilation, and complete self-denial.

Notes

The last line of the poem involves an elegant play on words. Táhirih refers to the universal Muslim declaration of faith (*shaháda*): "There is no god but God; Muhammad is the prophet of God." The believers are invited to insert themselves into the creed as the word "no" (or nothingness). The image is stunning—simultaneously a gesture of self-assertion and self-abnegation, faith and denial, affirmation and rejection.

The sixth line is missing in the Persian:

آیینه ای دان که تجلی در ا و
طلعت انوار الا میکند

In the seventh line which reads:

دیدن رویش فقرا را تمام
غرقه دریای فنا میکند

I suggest that there is an error in the text, and I propose that فنا (nothingness) be read as غنا (wealth). I must confess that this is what I usually decry in editors of Persian poetic works, i.e. the "correction" of a text in accordance with one's own judgment concerning errors that "must" have been made.

As it stands (before introducing my correction), a literal translation would read:

Seeing His face casts all the poor
drowning (*gharqe*) in the sea of nothingness (*faná*)

In the Arabic script, the initial forms of the letters "F" and "Gh" are (respectively) a closed and a partially open small circle with a superimposed dot. A copyist could easily have mixed the two. The word *ghaná* (wealth) not only

Amin Banani

gives the line a clearer meaning, it serves as a poetic artifice of alliteration with *gharqe* (drowning) in the same line.

Listen!
English Poem by Anthony A. Lee

طلعات قدسیین نثاری که جمال حق شده برملا

THIS POEM (p. 84) TAKES the form of a traditional ghazal, but the rhymes that Táhirih uses here are distinctive and arresting. In Persian, the rhymes make use of double vowels in the word endings:

> ... *barmala*
> ... *sala*
> ... *e'tela*

This allows the poet to bring the poem to a climax with its last word "Karbala," which is perhaps the most evocative word in the Shí'í vocabulary. The last line reads literally:

> I am the *shahanshah* of Karbala

(The word does not have a similar effect in English, and so the translation has not tried to preserve this element of the poem.) Karbala is, of course, the site of the martyrdom of Imam Husayn—the most revered figure of Shí'ih Islam and the focus of intense Shí'í piety.

This work is a straightforward declaration of the appearance of the Manifestation of God, and the specific reference here is to the Báb. The third stanza begins with the words, literally rendered:

> The everlasting beauty has appeared to raise the flag of the Bayán.

Notes

Yet, the poem also gives rise to a basic question: Who is speaking here? Whose voice is being heard? And, again, the question has no definitive answer.

The first three stanzas of the poem appear to be written in the voice of Táhirih herself, who proclaims and celebrates the Glad Tidings of the Báb. In the fourth stanza, she assumes the voice of the Manifestation, who congratulates and admonishes his followers. The final warning is fearsome:

> If someone should not obey me and not hold to the cord
>   of my protection,
> I shall distance him from my sanctuary and abandon him
>   in wrath to the wind of nothingness.

Immediately after, we hear a majestic and timeless voice. As the poem continues, we seem to hear the voice of Imam Husayn ("the Prince of Karbalá") and even the voice of God himself. There is a specific reference to the moment of pre-existence when God assembled all the unborn souls to witness to his Lordship. Powerfully, the poet calls on paradox and contradiction (manifest/hidden, timeless/placeless) to suggest spiritual states.

The voice of the poem throughout elides from that of Táhirih to that of God, from the human to the divine, from the earthly to the transcendent, from a specific announcement to a timeless truth. The effect is to build ecstatic declarations one upon another until the reader is caught up and lost in rapture.

Edward G. Browne translated a fragment of this poem, attributing it only doubtfully to Táhirih.[7] His translation reads:

Amin Banani

> *If anyone walks in my path I will cry to him that he may
> be warned
> That whoever becomes my lover shall not escape from
> sorrow and affliction.
> If anyone obeys me not and does not grasp the cord of
> my protection[8]
> I will drive him far from my sanctuary, I will cast him in
> wrath to the winds of "No."[9]
> I am Eternal from the Everlasting World; I am the One
> from the Realms of the Limitless;
> I am come [to seek for] the people of the Spirit, and
> towards me indeed do they advance.[10]*

Running After You

English Poem by Anthony A. Lee

THIS IS CERTAINLY one of Táhirih's most famous poems (p. 87). In fact, except for "Point by Point", it is her most famous poem. It is purportedly addressed to the king, Nasiru'd-Dín Shah, as her reply to his proposal of marriage (see pp. 26-28).

"Running After You" is supposed to be Táhirih's poetic reply. It was not unusual for educated Persians of the time to carry on a correspondence in verse. If the

---

7. From *Materials for the Study of the Bábí Religion* (Cambridge University Press, 1918) p. 352
8. Or Saintship, for *Wiláyat* has both meanings. Amongst the Arabs he who would seek the protection of some great Shaykh or Amir catches hold of one of the cords of his tent, crying *Aná dakhíluk!* "I place myself under thy protection!"—E.G.B.
9. Not-Being, or Negation, or Annihilation.—E.G.B.
10. The Arabic words with which this line concludes are, as is to often the case with the Bábís, hopelessly ungrammatical.—E.G.B.

Notes

king's proposal had been veiled in poetry; Táhirih's reply may have been similarly veiled. The poem begins with an Arabic phrase that evokes the most formal, classical form of Persian poetry. Literally translated, the poem begins:

> The magnetism of yearning for you binds with chains of sorrow and calamity . . .

But one must immediately admit that the reply is not very well veiled. Her rejection of the king's proposal is complete, almost contemptuous. We might say that the veil is removed halfway through the poem.

This poem was translated in full by Browne.[11] His version reads:

> *The thralls of yearning love constrain the bonds of pain and calamity.*
> *These broken-hearted lovers of thine to yield their lives in their zeal for thee.*[12]
> *Though with sword in hand my Darling stand with intent to slay though I sinless be,*
> *If it pleases him, this tyrant's whim, I am well content with his tyranny.*
> *As in sleep I lay at the break of day that cruel charmer came to me,*
> *And in the grace of his form and face the dawn of the morn I seem to see.*
> *The musk of Cathay might perfume gain from the scent of those fragrant tresses rain.*

---

11. Browne's translation and footnotes are taken from his publication of this poem in *Materials for the Study of the Bábí Religion* (Cambridge University Press, 1918) p. 348.
12. This poem is presumably addressed to the Báb.—E.G.B.

Amin Banani [handwritten]

While his eyes demolish a faith in vain attacked by the
  pagans of Tartary.[13]
With you, who condemn both love and wine[14] for the
  hermit's cell and the zealot's shrine,
What can I do, for our Faith divine you hold as a thing of
  infamy?
The tangled curls of thy darling's hair, and thy saddle and
  steed are thy only care;
In thy heart the Absolute hath no share, nor thought of the
  poor man's poverty.
Sikandar's[15] pomp and display be thine, the Qalandar's[16]
  habit and way be mine;
That, if it please thee, I resign, while this, though bad, is
  enough for me.
Pass from the station of "I" and "We," and choose for thy
  home Nonentity,
For when thou has done the like of this, thou shall reach
  the supreme Felicity.

Friends are Knocking at the Door [handwritten]

English Poem by Anthony A. Lee

در وصل تو میسّر شد احباب

THIS POEM (p. 89) is a ghazal composed with a simple meter and rhyme scheme. The double-vowel rhymes that the poet uses take full advantage of the music of the Persian language. In the first line, for example, *ahbáb* (friends) is rhymed with *abwáb* (doors, gates). Again, there is every indication that the poet intended this piece to be sung, rather than simply recited.

---

13. I.e. the religion of Islam, which, having survived the terrible Tartar or Mongol invasion of the thirteenth century, fell before the Báb.—E.G.B.
14. "Love and wine" are to be understood here in a mystical sense.—E.G.B.
15. Alexander the Great.—E.G.B.
16. A *Qalandar* is a kind of *darwish* or religious mendicant.—E.G.B.

Notes

The first line of the poem is half-Arabic and half-Persian. This half-and-half, bilingual pattern (*molamma'*) is maintained throughout the first seven lines of the poem. The next three lines are Persian, but, the poem ends with a final bilingual line.

This fractured structure reinforces the duality that stands at the core of the poem. A multitude of yearning friends are knocking at the door of the Beloved, and the door is locked. The pleading voices of the lovers are cut off from the object of their desire. Separation and estrangement rule their condition. The poet begs for the Beloved to open the gates (*abwáb*, the plural form of *báb*). She asks him to remove his veils (*hejab* and *negáb*). Here we see again the motif of the removal of veils that is found in a number of Táhirih's poems.

Finally, the poem shifts into Persian. The pleaders and the Beloved become merged together in a remarkably egalitarian union of master and slave. Here we witness the reversal of the normal order, as the wise are struck dumb, fools find wisdom, etc. This reversal is a common feature of classical Persian poetry as a representation of the ultimate mystical condition of union.

I Am Lost
English Poem by Jascha Kessler

THIS IS ANOTHER ghazal (p. 92) that, in form, tone, and content, is written as a mystic love song. This is a classical poetic form. In this poem, we hear the voice of the poet pining and pleading, making the familiar complaints of the cruelty of the Beloved and the pain of separation.

Amin Banani

In the last few lines of the poem, Táhirih echoes an erotic image found in one of the most famous poems of Hafez. Often thought of as a Sufi mystic, Hafez was no such thing. Many of his poems are frankly skeptical. In the famous poem he wrote for his epitaph, however, he makes a genuine plea for some kind of mystical union, while avoiding formalized Sufi language. Hafez writes:

> Although I am old, clasp me tight in your arms one night
> so that at dawn I will rise from your embrace young again.
>
> I am a bird of heaven mired in this world,
> but in union with you, I will take wing again.

Táhirih's lines also avoid Sufi formulae. They read literally:

> Step into my bed this early morning.
> Out of your bounty and generosity,
>
> and the desire to be near you,
> I shall take flight on both my wings.

This Heart
English Poem by Anthony A. Lee

بخیالست ای نکورو مبیسد ام باشد این دل

THIS IS ANOTHER GHAZAL (p. 95) with simple meter and rhyme that is very suitable for musical rendition. A simple mono-rhyme is maintained throughout the piece.

The poet's own heart, "this heart" (*in del*), speaks as the voice of the poem. By the end, the reader has run the gamut of sentiment and emotion that flows out from that heart. The heart is moved to speak; then it is shredded

Notes

bloody. Again, it is restored in contemplation of the majesty of the Beloved. The heart is agitated, made firm, driven from everything, attracted to its Beloved, freed from death, consumed by fire.

Finally, the poem concludes:

> From my heart, flames rise up because it is kin to the fire.
> Why should it not bear fruit and be fulfilled?

No One Else
English Poem by Jascha Kessler

غیر او مشهود نبود در عیان

THIS POEM (p. 95) is written in mathnavi form, that is, in rhymed couplets. This is a poetic form normally used in Persian literature for narrative poems, rather than for love poems. Nonetheless, this is a declaration of devotion that is replete with theological reference in a Bábí context.

The poet also refers to other Prophets of God in the Bábí belief system—the reference to the Bayán (the Báb's holy book) in the first line, for instance. The second line makes reference to both Moses and Muhammad in a play on words. According to scripture, one of the proofs of Moses was that he pulled a leprous hand from out of his sleeve, then returned it and pulled it out again healed. (Exodus 4:6-7; Qur'an 20:23, 28:33) In addition, the Qur'an is referred to in Islam as the "proof" (*forqán*) of Muhammad. The second line reads literally:

> The name of God was proven by him who was given that name.
> The proof of God came forth from the sleeve.

Amin Banani

Significantly, in this poem, Táhirih repeatedly makes use of the Arabic word *bahá* (glory) as a personal name, rather than an abstract concept. So, it would be quite difficult to miss the direct references to Bahá'u'lláh in this poem, as well.

From Those Locks
English Poem by Jascha Kessler

ای به سر زلف تو سودای من

HAD NO OTHER poem of Táhirih's survived except this one (p. 102), it would have been enough to establish her place among the highest rank of the Persian metaphysical poets. We might regard this work as one of her most accomplished masterpieces.

The theme of the poem is simple and straightforward, without literary complexity. It reads easily—with no Arabic phrases, difficult words, or obscure references. But the verse reveals layers of meaning, deep themes, multiple cultural and literary references. The form of the poem is almost perfectly harmonized and united with these layers of meaning. Throughout, the poet is able to maintain a marvelous tension between the traditional forms and images of classical Persian poetry and the innovative thrust of her own message.

The poem takes the form of a *tarji'band mokhammas* (a rondo in five-line clusters). This is a musical form that lends itself to song. There are eighteen stanzas of five lines each. Within each stanza, the first four lines repeat a single rhyme—while the fifth line uses a different rhyme that returns at the fifth line of each stanza.

This poetic form is not rare, but it was not commonly used in the Persian classical tradition. However, Táhirih's

Notes

rondo has an important and well-known precursor that she was certainly aware of—a poem by the seventeenth-century Persian poet Hatef. His work was intended as a pious, Muslim polemic written to reject the Christian doctrine of the Holy Trinity. In Hatef's poem, he carries on an argument with a Christian nun concerning the unity of God and the falseness of Christian doctrine. She uses every argument to convince him, and he is almost seduced by her beauty. But, at the climax of his poem, Hatef hears the church bells ring—and, in his mind, he can hear them chanting the Muslim creed: "There is no God but God. Muhammad is the Prophet of God." So, he is called back to the true faith and rejects Christian heresies.

Any reader educated in the Persian poetic tradition would immediately be reminded of Hatef's poem upon reading this work by Táhirih. However, in deliberate contrast, she uses her poem to affirm the unity and oneness of all religions. Beyond this general statement, she also makes a deeply moving personal statement of self-annihilation—the merger of "I" and "Thou."

The tone of this poem is ecstatic from the very first line; and its passion, immediacy, and devotion rise continually until the end. The poem opens with an evocative call to the Beloved that delineates a clear distinction between the poet and the one she addresses. This duality is maintained for four lines of the first stanza, and then resolved in the fifth line. This pattern is repeated throughout the poem until the end.

Kessler's rendition of this poem in English translation captures the high tone and formal structure of Táhirih's original. He has also retained the poem's rhyme scheme in the English, which is a remarkable accomplishment. However, in the original, the fifth line of every stanza ends

Amin Banani

with the Persian word *man* (meaning, *I* or *me*). That element of the poem gives the original an intense resonance, since the word continually returns at the end of each stanza. This device also reinforces the theme of the poem—tension between "I" and "Thou"—without unnecessary decoration or artificial literary locutions. The end rhyme is *-an*, which produces the clash of an open vowel and a resonant consonant. Beyond this, since *man* is a two-letter word in Persian (the vowel is not written), the reader is repeatedly reminded of duality.

The first stanza opens with a call that evokes an image of the twisted and disheveled hair of the Beloved, which is compared to the mad passion of the lover. Next, the poet describes the red lips of her Beloved. So, we are immediately plunged into the full-bodied images of erotic love from the first lines of the poem.

In the second stanza, the remarkable sensuality of the poem returns to the Beloved's lips as the source of salvation. The fifth line reads literally:

>... your lips are my messiah

It is more common, in classical Persian poems, for the poet to evoke the more polite image of the "breath" of the Messiah as the instrument of salvation. But here Táhirih deliberately chooses a more immediate, corporeal metaphor—rather than the distant and abstract image of "breath." This brazen and electrifying sensuality is maintained throughout the piece.

The third stanza reinforces the opposition of "I" and "Thou" which is the poem's focus. Táhirih raises the tension of the poem in the fifth line with a question. Literally:

Notes

> If you are me, then what is this shape [of my body]?

The fourth stanza involves a play on words and images. The Persian word *mehr* can mean both "sun" and "love," and is derived from Mithra, the name of the Iranian sun-god of prehistoric times. The first line then reads literally:

> I have been reduced to the low state of an atom
> by your *mehr*

Evoking the traditional metaphors of wine, hair, and passion, the fourth line startles the reader with the statement, literally:

> . . . since you are me, I have become a self-worshipper
> (*khod-parast*)

This last word normally conveys a negative meaning of *selfish* or *egotistical*. But here, the poet has transformed the word and made it an emblem of selfless devotion.

The fifth stanza begins with more questions, which express the tortured separation of lover and Beloved, "I" and "Thou." Again, the fifth line resolves the separation. A literal translation here would read:

> If this heart is yours, why do you bloody it?
> If not yours, why do you drive it mad with love?
> You increase the fire in my heart breath by breath,
> until you have driven away all my selfness.
>   Take your place in my raptured heart.

The sixth stanza presents the reader with a bold, even shocking, statement that flies in the face of Muslim orthodoxy. Literally:

Amin Banani

> When the fire of your love flamed up,
> it burned away from me both heathen and Muslim.
> So now I bow myself down before the arch of your eyebrow.

The final line of the stanza forcefully asserts the unity of religions:

> There is no difference between Ka'aba and church

Here Hatef's poem is immediately brought to mind. Hatef's intention was to insist on precisely this difference—with Islam affirmed and the Christian church rejected. Táhirih fearlessly asserts the opposite message.

In the seventh stanza, Táhirih compares the divine act of creation with putting pen to paper—as in writing a poem. This image can also be found in some of the poems of Rumi and Hafez. The creative act of poetry is equated with God's act of creating the universe. Here pen and paper embrace in an erotic union—also a creative act, of course. The last line of the stanza can be literally translated:

> From eternity your love was in my raptured heart

This line suggests the well-known tradition attributed to the Prophet Muhammad (*hadith qodsí*) in which, speaking with the voice of God, he says: "I was a Hidden Treasure, and I loved to be known. Therefore I created all things to know me." We might also be reminded of a passage (written years later) from Bahá'u'lláh's Hidden Words: "I loved thy creation, hence I created thee."

The eighth stanza continues the juxtaposition of "I" and "Thou." It reads literally:

Notes

> When the hand of destiny mixed the clay of Adam,
> it planted your love in the field of my breast.
> Your love became my destiny.
> Now I am free of hell and heaven.
> > I have no desire except for you.

The ninth stanza reads literally:

> I am both eternal and ephemeral.
> Of myself I take a taste of divine wine.
> I am burned up in the valley of perplexity.
> I am traveling in the desert of bewilderment.
> > What will happen to this disgraced heart of mine?

The first line of the tenth stanza makes reference to the day of preexistence (*alast*) when God gathered all the unborn souls and caused them to acknowledge his Lordship. Since that time, the poet says she has become lost in the noise and tumult of the world. But lover and Beloved are again united in the fifth line, which reads:

> I became the heart, and He the heart's adornment

In the eleventh stanza, Táhirih plays with images of the sacred and the profane—as she has throughout the poem. The body of the Beloved becomes the sacred place. She repeats the image of her Beloved's eyebrow as the arch that marks the *qiblih* (the direction of prayer). This play culminates in the fifth line, which reads:

> The locks of your hair are my cross in the convent

Here the Christian image harkens back to Hatef. But it would have been a shocking line of poetry in the nine-

Amin Banani

teenth-century Muslim society in which Táhirih lived—a line guaranteed to scandalize the orthodox.

The twelfth stanza contains in the first line a direct reference to the Báb, who was known to the Bábís as Hadrat-i 'Alá' (His Holiness the Exalted One). The stanza reads literally:

> I am absolutely enamored of Hadrat-i 'Alá.
> I love to see that beloved face.
> I travel in that valley of passion.
> I let go of all else but you.
> > All my limbs are filled with your love.

The thirteenth stanza begins to bring the poem to its conclusion, as Táhirih expresses her dissatisfaction and impatience with separation. She asks:

> How long do I have to listen to wise counsel?
> How long to I have to hide my agitation?
> How long must I stay silent in separation?

The fourteenth stanza, then, answers the questions posed in the previous one:

> I will throw away robe and prayer rug.
> I will pour wine into a crystal cup
> and cause the fire of Mt. Sinai to flash . . .

The fifteenth stanza reads literally:

> Love planted its flag at my ruined house,
> and greeted me at the gate.
> It poured the wine of God in my cup.
> Now I am an outsider to myself and to everyone else.
> > God requires of me my highest effort.

Notes

The sixteenth stanza returns to the image of the call of God on the day of preexistence:

> When the cupbearer at the Feast of *Alast*
> poured wine into everyone's cup,
> every atom was brought low.
> The wine itself got drunk on me,
>   from the effect of my love.

Up until the seventeenth stanza, there has been a clear apposition of love and Beloved in the first four lines—with some kind of union of the two suggested in the fifth line. Now, to end the poem, Táhirih abandons this structure. In the seventeenth stanza, only the Beloved is heard speaking, and the poet's voice is silent:

> Love raises its call at every instant
> and says to all living things:
> Whoever wants to come in my direction
> cannot hope to avoid calamity
>   but will set foot on the shores of my ocean.

In the eighteenth and last stanza of the poem, it is only the voice of the lover-poet that is heard speaking. Finally, all separation is resolved. Táhirih calls on the image of the Indian slave at the gates of a Persian city. Indian (that is, gypsy) musicians would often play at sunrise and at sunset above the city gates. And she describes herself as one of these:

> I am the Hindu slave keeping time at the gate.
> I am the lost bird in your snare.
> I am the bird of the night that hangs down—
> erased from myself and living in your name,
>   removed from me the pain of I and we.